WHEN WE EXHALE

An Anthology of Black Women: Rooted in ancestral medicine

Edited by Alie Jones, Danielle Mason, & Janae Newsom

BFP
BLACK FREIGHTER PRESS

San Francisco, California

https://www.blackfreighterpress.com/

CONTENTS

Foreword by Jeneé Darden   7

Introduction by Alie Jones, Danielle Mason, & Janae Newsom   11

"When We Exhale" by Dr. Ayodele Nzinga   15

PART I: GRIEF REST INTIMACY

"Our Grandmothers" by Maya Angelou   19

"The Body Prophetic" by Atena O. Danner   24

"A Hot Bath" by Aáron Breanna Heard   25

"the minutiae of my chaos starts with coffee" by Raychelle Heath   26

"Sweet Grief" by Aáron Breanna Heard   27

"Sea Salt Soaks" by Amber D. Dodd   29

"about grief" by Nicole Morris   33

"godspeed, glore" by Jasmine Knowles   34

"Revolutionaries I can't trust" by Brandy Collins   35

"No Poems Today" by Aáron Breanna Heard   36

"How to Learn the Wrong Way to Grieve" by Maya Williams   37

"My Dad is waiting to welcome me" by Loraine Masiya Mponela   38

"A Womb Story" by Sherniece Johnson Smith   39

"Let love" by Daad Sharfi   42

"Memory" by Kimani Rose   43

"defeat your vanity" by Raina J. León   44

"fly girl" by Karla Tiffany   45

"on the topic of:" by Ayodele Nzinga   47

"Peach River Prayer" by Kenia D. Hale   49

"Your Queendom Calls" by dr. adrienne danyelle oliver   53

"Metta to Our Healing" by Sarai Bordeaux   55

"Checkmate" by Felicia Johnson   57

"I dare you" by Alie Jones   58

"Sag Cider" by Raheem Divine   60

"My Kind" by M. Nzadi Keita   61

"By Breath or By Prayer" by Yeva Johnson   64

"Grief Meditation (Double Sonku)" by Julia Mallory   65

"ANCESTOR" by Natachi Mez   66

PART II: INTIMACY GRIEF REST

"Kaleidoscope" by Sonia Sanchez   68

"THE DANDELION RITUAL" by Lyn Patterson   69

"When You See a Black Woman Pass You on the
   Street" by Kelechi Ubozoh   70

"THE MOTHER OF ALL JAMS" by Tawhida Tanya Evanson   71

"That Special Recipe from Grandmothers and their Mothers
   Too" by Yeva Johnson   72

"Good Morning, Heartache" by Danielle Mason   73

"Spirit Break" by Daya Stanley   75

"home is where the heart is" by Mallessa James   76

"Dream with me" by Zhalisa Clarke   78

"Salt Water Mumbo Jumbo" by Karla Clark   80

"stone throat" by Raina J. León   81

"Moon Child" by Raheem Divine   83

"They Were Right" by Clinnesha D. Sibley   84

"Everybody's Voice Got a Little Something In It" by Julia Mallory   86

"Lay all that mess down: A Story of Black Maternal Loss,
   "Survival, & Liberation" by Ebony Lumumba   88

"For Auntie" by Kisaye Natsuki   91

"Supernova" by Victoria Moten   93

"When Someone You Know Dies by Suicide Again" by Maya Williams   95

"Day 3" by Felicia Johnson   96

"Why We Nod at Each Other (A folktale)" by Meilan Carter-Gilkey   97

"Emotional Junkfood" by Rowana Abbensetts-Dobson   99

"All the Benches in Manhattan Have Ghosts in Their
   Wood" by Chelsea Williams   100

"You" by Whylde Chylde   101

"Janet Jackson Wants to Dance with Me" by Suzi Q. Smith   102

"The Floral Pedestal" by Shamoiya Washington   104

"Some Old Havoc" by Ciera Javae   105

PART III: REST INTIMACY GRIEF

"In Memoriam: Rev. Martin Luther King, Jr. (Part I)" by June Jordan   108

"I am by Ariel Ward 110   109

"A Recipe for Exhale C.A.K.E." by dr. adrienne danyelle oliver   110

"My Exhale Releases the Pain" by Sonnie Dae   112

"Little Sorrow" by Danielle Shaleece   113

"Evermore" by Alie Jones   114

"Carolina Gold Mississippi Blue (3)" by Constance Collier-Mercado   115

"When I Stopped Running From My Mother I
     Exhaled" by Jeanine DeHoney   116

"Jan 24" by Karla Brundage   120

"My Marrow" by Asantewaa Boykin   121

"WE MOVE TO MILITANT LOVE, DON'T WE?" by Daad Sharfi   122

"I am the river" by Raychelle Heath   123

"untitled futures" by shah noor hussein   124

"duality" by Kimani Rose   126

"and maybe Mother Earth is an angry Black woman, too" by Mallessa James 127

"In Memoriam" by Maya Williams   128

"Processing Grief: A Meditation" by RR Scott   129

"Invoice" by Joyce Lee   131

"That Time I Felt the Sun" by Janae Newsom   132

"Unbreakable" by Kelechi Ubuzoh   133

"In the day diamonds are in the water" by Nia Pearl   135

FOREWORD

Black women have long had a wonderful and powerful way with words when it comes to affirming ourselves. Sojourner Truth let it be known in 1851 that Black women deserve rights in her speech "Ain't I a Woman?" Three queer sistas ignited a global movement by simply proclaiming "Black Lives Matter." Beyonce's song title "Break My Soul" is an affirmation for people when folks aren't treating them right on the job and in their personal lives. And how many of us feel stronger and sexier after reciting Maya Angelou's "Phenomenal Woman"? That's because words are more than, well, words. As Angelou said, "Words are things. They get on the walls… and your clothes, and finally into you."

I know the positive difference words make when they seep into your heart. My grandmother is an ancestor. When I feel hopeless, I can still hear her sweet Mississippi drawl, "Baby, prayer changes things." Every once and a while, I open a jar on my altar filled with colorful scraps of paper. Each piece has a quote from a person who said something kind to me. Those memories of kindness make me smile. For those moments I need to shut out the world and wrap myself in a blanket of loving words, I light a few candles pop in my old Anita Baker CDs and wander in her lyrics.

When We Exhale: Reflections on Rest, Grief and Intimacy is a beautiful offering by Black women writers whose words settle in your spirit. In this literary respite Black women writers have opened their hearts, mirroring their experiences, so other Black women can see themselves. The writings are salves for emotional wounds such as longing and regret. Some are eulogies in memory of a loved one or a womb removed for health reasons. There are recipes for joy in times of peace and distress. Mantras and prayers when in need of radical self-love and relaxation. Black women are not just bringing receipts, but invoicing society for our contributions and pain in a world that we've given so much to. There are declarations of our wonder and power. While other pages give warm embraces through the writers' memories of pleasure and love in various forms. The tones of each piece range from soft to fiery, but all possess a special tenderness that sometimes Black women forget we can tap into.

Just as a deep breath relaxes the body and releases toxins, *When We Exhale* bestows healing. The anthology's theme is timely as many Black breaths have been stolen through violence and the COVID pandemic. Add to that Black women dealing with misogynoir, our families, jobs, relationships, inflation, high gas prices, climate change and saving our democracy. No wonder many of us are navigating the world with shallow breaths and tight shoulders. Black women are often expected to dig our feet into the ground, hold our breath and stand firm in the storm. *When We Exhale* hits the pause button on that thinking and brings us back to the center. The writers' openness in this book encourages Black women to put down the unreasonable weight of expectations placed on our shoulders; breathe and find the liberation within to feel and express ourselves.

Something beautiful happens when Black women gather and we give ourselves the gift of vulnerability. Whether that gathering is in person or between a book jacket. *When We Exhale* is a magical, literary space that honors the sacredness of Black women's experiences, and shows us grace as we process grief, intimacy and our need for rest. I invite you to relax. As you read, let the words pour into you. Welcome love. Release your tears. Delight in arousal. Laugh. Be empowered. Heal. Remember to breathe in, and out…deeply.

Jeneé Darden

INTRODUCTION

When We Exhale is an Anthology of Black Women rooted in ancestral medicine. With over fifty submissions from Women of the African Diaspora, healers, storytellers, educators, and activists. This collection of poems, essays, meditations, recipes, and short stories from Black women reflects on rest, grief, and intimacy. As editors we made a decision to weave the themes together like a braid. We acknowledge that life has grief intertwined with intimacy and glimmers of joy. We are calling in spaces of rest and support for Black women. Real support and genuine connection. Many of the Black women writers we love and look up to did not receive their flowers while they could smell them. This collection carves out space for multitudes and collective reverence.

Grief is for the living and the dead. Chilling, masterful, painful. The writing in this anthology is an exploration of grief as memory, hope, a wish, a promise, and a curse. Black women make magic happen in our homes and our hearts, mending together with each exhale. At the altar of vulnerability and despair we surrender. We sob for those we've lost and loved. For those we will never know and still love. In these stories we see grief through the eyes of lovers, mothers, cousins, friends, children. We accept that grief can look and feel different, we acknowledge that grief is a necessary conduit which acts as a shield, a covering, a shelter.

These passages of poems, stories, essays, and meditations that are gutting and unapologetically sincere. Each piece takes hold of the reader through the magic of surrendering to sorrow. These pieces speak to the inner sentiments of all who have experienced loss, longing, and love. These stories make legs and stand, these stories are grief work in motion. These words make grief medicine.

The featured works around Intimacy invoke the spirit of belonging within the interior worlds of Black women, interrogating functions of desire and possession found in the grasp of one's identity, interpersonal relationships, and place in the outside world. This theme explores stillness, silence, and the intimacy found in being alone; the liminal space between sound & surrender, and questions one must ask when navigating the remnants of loss. How might intimacy be found in the level of care given to one's spiritual fulfillment?

Together we explore the possibility for support to be found in ritual and the power to conjure alternate identities for ourselves. Intimacy allows one to step outside of misery and claim a persona that eradicates it. Many of the featured works reckon with the crosses that Black women bear, things that often go unsaid, and yet, are carried and felt anyway, opening the dialogue regarding resilience in spite of trauma, one's personal power to heal, and the intimacy of connection to spirit guides.

We journey through the sensory experiences of the body and flesh. Here we explore the sweet and tender, soft and supple nature of intimacy, spanning the internal dialogue of welcoming in a new lover, to the enchanting and sensuous nature of lovemaking. To taste, touch, smell, and drink fully from the wellspring of one's desires, honors the level of communion engaged in the act of intimacy. We welcome in the seductress and the enchanteur, the black magic woman into this cypher, whose charms and charisma can outwit any attempts of violation.

We honor the tenderness found within an individual's connection to the outside world–the narratives that loom and linger, shaping one's commitment to their communities and sense of self. There is a deep level of vulnerability found in the developmental process of becoming, in which claiming an identity for ourselves is often based upon proximity to cultural and familial traditions that inspire us to *be*. Intimacy in this anthology explores the inheritance of memory, and how intimacy with the imagination, and belief in the futurity of our desires, gives us purpose. The quiet between these lines also can serve as a reminder to surrender and trust what's to come. Intimacy initiates us into the safety found within the sacred. We are holy and holding.

Alie Jones, Danielle Mason, & Janae Newsom

If you are silent about your pain, they'll kill you and say you enjoyed it.

—Zora Neale Hurston

When We Exhale
Dr. Ayodele Nzinga

when we exhale
we will become proficient
in open ended lucid dreams
that finally leave the middle passage
we will weave
tomorrow with ancestral authority
when
we exhale
fruit will grow fruit
again
new language will be born
to explain
rain finding her season
again
honey bees will return
the rhythm of our days
will remember us
softly
like mamas' arms
we rise
mist over water
stars freckled across
ebony skies
we are
creations daughters
remembering
the dream before
the need to
overcome

became

she is

we are

dahomey's

rose petal garden

the return of eden

liberty

unchained

alive

on arrival no

weapon formed

#manifestinghere

when we exhale

the band will play

above the noise of

a million

or

more

smooth black

grannies

shouting

on the head of

a pin

cause they prayers

finally

came true

PART I:
GRIEF REST INTIMACY

Our Grandmothers
Maya Angelou

She lay, skin down in the moist dirt,
the canebrake rustling
with the whispers of leaves, and
loud longing of hounds and
the ransack of hunters crackling the near
branches.

She muttered, lifting her head a nod toward
freedom,
I shall not, I shall not be moved.

She gathered her babies,
their tears slick as oil on black faces,
their young eyes canvassing mornings of madness.
Momma, is Master going to sell you
from us tomorrow?

Yes.
Unless you keep walking more
and talking less.
Yes.
Unless the keeper of our lives
releases me from all commandments.
Yes.
And your lives,
never mine to live,
will be executed upon the killing floor of
innocents.
Unless you match my heart and words,
saying with me,

I shall not be moved.

In Virginia tobacco fields,
leaning into the curve
of Steinway
pianos, along Arkansas roads,
in the red hills of Georgia,
into the palms of her chained hands, she
cried against calamity,
You have tried to destroy me
and though I perish daily,

I shall not be moved.

Her universe, often
summarized into one black body
falling finally from the tree to her feet,
made her cry each time into a new voice.
All my past hastens to defeat,
and strangers claim the glory of my love,
Iniquity has bound me to his bed.

yet, I must not be moved.

She heard the names,
swirling ribbons in the wind of history:
nigger, nigger bitch, heifer,
mammy, property, creature, ape, baboon,
whore, hot tail, thing, it.
She said, But my description cannot
fit your tongue, for
I have a certain way of being in this world,

and I shall not, I shall not be moved.

No angel stretched protecting wings
above the heads of her children,
fluttering and urging the winds of reason
into the confusions of their lives.
The sprouted like young weeds,
but she could not shield their growth
from the grinding blades of ignorance, nor
shape them into symbolic topiaries.
She sent them away,
underground, overland, in coaches and
shoeless.

When you learn, teach.
When you get, give.
As for me,

I shall not be moved.

She stood in midocean, seeking dry land.
She searched God's face.
Assured,
she placed her fire of service
on the altar, and though
clothed in the finery of faith,
when she appeared at the temple door,
no sign welcomed
Black Grandmother, Enter here.

Into the crashing sound,
into wickedness, she cried,

No one, no, nor no one million
ones dare deny me God, I go forth
along, and stand as ten thousand.

The Divine upon my right
impels me to pull forever
at the latch on Freedom's gate.

The Holy Spirit upon my left leads my
feet without ceasing into the camp of the
righteous and into the tents of the free.

These momma faces, lemon-yellow, plum-purple,
honey-brown, have grimaced and twisted
down a pyramid for years.
She is Sheba the Sojourner,
Harriet and Zora,
Mary Bethune and Angela,
Annie to Zenobia.

She stands
before the abortion clinic,
confounded by the lack of choices.
In the Welfare line,
reduced to the pity of handouts.
Ordained in the pulpit, shielded
by the mysteries.
In the operating room,
husbanding life.
In the choir loft,
holding God in her throat.
On lonely street corners,

hawking her body.
In the classroom, loving the
children to understanding.

Centered on the world's stage,
she sings to her loves and beloveds,
to her foes and detractors:
However I am perceived and deceived,
however my ignorance and conceits,
lay aside your fears that I will be undone,

for I shall not be moved.

The Body Prophetic

Atena O. Danner

There's a kind of crying so intense that it changes your voice.
Quenches and tempers your trembling reeds, so when you sing,
It's the hot, shaking song of the broken open.

Tripping bass of continents shifting over ages, under oceans
Pulsing of roots cradling the ancient, cycling breath of trees
Crackling collective of hearts: the friction of every growing thing

The body fallen into tears and the ache of unending laughter
Each carry the same revelation.

A Hot Bath

Aáron Breanna Heard

I stepped through hot water and into myself
        Here I return to womb and return to trust
        Here I release and connect and hear clearly

        Without cover, unpeeled
        I am naked and convening
                    Close to the other side
        I sit still and open
        In reverence
        Revealing myself tender

When and where do you allow yourself to fall off the bone?

        I make a soup of my flesh
        A broth of my shedding
        I make of myself a soothing for my ancestors
        They make of me a balm for most hearts

        The only place consistently safe and consistently mine
        A hot bath
        A tender heart
        Untethered in time

the minutiae of my chaos starts with coffee

Raychelle Heath

the minutiae of my chaos starts with coffee
black
and a sink full of dishes that are a handy distraction
from the deadline that pulses just beneath my right eye

down to my shaking fingers

coffee with a bit of turmeric and cardamom
pour over
into the deep green mouth of my only mug
not like the stacks on stacks of emails that boldly list their demands
for me to
check my calendar

check my wallet

check my brain
do you remember what it's like to drink coffee
slowly so that it doesn't burn the tongue
slowly so you can taste the monte

the hands that picked the berries
the moment of drying
of roasting
of grinding
I check my jaw, move my tongue
from the roof of my mouth
relax
focus on my breath
rising falling
rising falling

remember to light your candle today
remember to place a bit of incense
remember to face yourself in the mirror
remember to say I love you
slowly
s t r e t c h i n g
out the each letter
with your lips and tongue

Sweet Grief

Aáron Breanna Heard

Sadness
Crept Up
On me
Like a gnat

On a sweet thing.

I swat it away-
For now.
Knowing she'll be back
Knowing her visits are necessary
Knowing her presence tells me
I am here.

*and by 10, I'd considered better ways to lose a Black mother. from old age or maybe even death on impact. my mother could have died on January 8, 2006, but we couldn't let her die until July 17, 2013. at 10, I didn't realize I'd ask my mother to stay and suffer for me, again. despite the 10 centimeters dilated, the contractions, the pushing-with-no-epidural, I asked her to stretch herself upon a hospital bed, again. this time not for 20 hours, but for 7 years.

Briana grogan

Sea Salt Soaks

Amber D. Dodd

"On three."

One. Two. Thr

My piercer dug into my right nostril with sterling silver in February. My body did not respond to the foreign object until May. Unlike my healthy stretched earlobes decorated with titanium tunnels, red, blackened, scar tissue throbbed and pulsated like sci-fi fetuses to engulf my nose stud. I texted my classmate Kamien, who adorned his face and ears with seven, thriving piercings, in a hurry over my keloid staging a dermal mutiny.

"My ex's did the same," He explained.

"What did she do to heal it?!"

"Kept it clean with soap and she put pure sea salt and water solution on it." Sea salt is unrefined, hand-harvested and solar dried. It is used to escort dirt out of pores, jumpstart skin cells and decontaminate infections through its purified salinity. I went to the market and grabbed a pound of it to begin the sodium chloride ritual.

Pour ¼ teaspoon of sea salt into a cup. Add lukewarm water to the salt, returning it to oceanic antiquity. Dunk your infected area in for ten minutes. Wipe away crusted and dead skin with a q-tip. Repeat until the area is clean and skin stretchy.

Soaks continued throughout my two-week trip to New York City. I participated in the New York Times' Student Journalism Institute. Twenty-six college students across America were handpicked to write, research and report while supervised under the world's top journalists.

I rubbed my stretched ears after dumping saltwater full of dead skin cells in my hotel bathroom. The ear holes, big as pupils, sizzled as sea salt residue invaded its raw skin, so I soaked them too, finishing with a concoction of shea butter and jojoba oil. My keloid shrunk and ears healed as did my ignorant journalism practices.

I started arriving long before our 9:30 a.m. start to munch on organic grapefruits and fresh daily papers. I stopped taking story ideas from Twitter and found them through independent research. I listened. Executive editor Dean Banquet advised us to lean into what you're good at. Journalist Devin Gonzalez always chose strength in the tug-of-war between it and adversity. Pulitzer prize distributor Dana Canedy said to own our success.

These healthy habits exposed two things. One: My piercer did not educate me on the powers of sea salt during infection. Two: My unclear future in journalism is that I do not have one.

It is not that journalism is bland or tedious or boring. I cannot dig into journalism like my piercer or my mind for adequate creative nonfiction. I am an artist unwrapping literary gifts in inappropriate settings like that unfit profession. The career epiphany marked my Manhattan departure as my jewelry lay evenly on my nose.

***

Magnesium sulfate, better known as Epsom salt, is a saline laxative. Many suggest you drink the salt to experience its healing powers. Grab a cup. No more than three teaspoons of Epsom salt. Add lemon and eight ounces of warm water. Stir. Experience the periodic table's saline solution and perform internal magic tricks. Since God's flowers require sun and rain, I simply soaked in it.

Scoop two cups for every gallon to effectively soak for soreness, sprains, and bruises. Crumbs of the crystallized batter will morph into saline waterfalls in ivory bathtubs. I try to submerge my problems.

Sometimes it is not enough.

Depths of the world felt fickle at my eighteen-year-old fingertips. I managed a peace treaty between surviving freshman year, raging hormones, and low self-esteem for my first experience at self-confidence. I felt alive during the summer graveyard shifts, meeting my middle school crush AJ for backdoor car rendezvous. He performed mind-blowing oral sex on me right before my sophomore year started. Life-changing, if you will.

AJ hosted my going away party, inviting two bite marks to redesign my vaginal insides. I wrapped four smile-shaped ice cubes in a pink rag to press against the deep lacerations. This soreness could be soaked away, I thought. Then I starved myself to avoid urinating. It bothered me to sweat. It bothered me to breathe. It bothered me to think.

My mother would fill the tub with warm water.

"Try soaking in some Epsom salt," She suggested. "It won't burn so bad." The warm jacuzzi buzzed upon my tender, sore skin. Soft translucent crystals grew into waterproof samurai swords, slashing at my thighs and pelvic area. Peeing was only fifteen seconds. It was a lifetime of pain.

Four days later in the gynecologist office, a woman next to me rubbed her stretched stomach as unborn limbs poked its nutritious shelter. She looked down and gracefully smiled. I assumed she was ready to hear newborn cries that signaled its beginning humanity. That it was alive.

As my body rested upon the teal, plastic practice table, Dr. Pernickle fetched a silver instrument to scrap my labia. My responsive squeaks harmonized my sensitivity. "Ahhhhh," She said, discovering a diagnosis through her single microscopic lens. "This is just herpes."

My mother heard her daughter's screams in heartbreak. Her arm-wide preserve could not protect me from how heavy the world reweighed.

"I am so, so sorry," Pernickle tried to comfort me. "When he bit you, each and every single bacterium in his mouth, every nook and cranny, went directly into your bloodstream. It was in you at the bite."

I assume AJ did not mean to shift my new sense of sexuality. That it had died. These were not lesions I could soak away.

***

Human tears contain water, lipids, glucose and an average six milligrams of sodium per tear. Crying releases natural painkillers such as leucine enkephalin, a morphine-like reaction toward your opioid receptors. It is the good feeling of empty exhaustion after a cry session, the warm blanket during a cry-nap.

Crying is our bodies' way of communicating emotional processes. It's a response to diverse emotions on the spectrum such as anger, pain, and sometimes, happiness. My reluctance of emotion, or lack thereof, chained me to just anger or sarcasm, so I avoided my face soaked in tears for years. Then I went to college 1,000 miles away from home.

I was either crying too little, too long, or for the wrong reasons. I sobbed for three hours over a boy. I could not weep in a five-minute recess over failed exams. I "sucked it up" by senior year. Instead of crying, I would vent to my new friend, Zamir. He became the safety net of emotional venting sessions from police reports, eviction notices, and other tactics used to keep me in collegiate hell.

The emotional burden of NAACP presidency with a lazy, backstabbing executive board, aftermaths of splitting with the potential love of my life, and shattering multiple hearts to move forward, being accused of passing my Epsom salt incident to someone, and roommates who called the cops on me for using marijuana as a coping mechanism hardened me back into a human house of stone. Graduation did the work of emotional demolition.

Z was there the night after graduation. It was the final night in my apartment before I returned home to Maryland. My other close friends Na'im, Sidney, Davondre, Kristen, and Jeltz came too, masking their sad goodbyes in a going away packing party. Tumbling boxes and stretched tape blended with blasting music and chatter during the Uno tournament. The sour stench of marijuana stung our noses, distracting us while I washed the remainder of my clothes and packed my room up. It was time for them to go by 2:40 a.m. We took our final group photos while tears blurred my eyes. I said my personal, choked up goodbyes and sent everyone on their way. Z stayed and walked me back into my empty apartment.

"I just know you not okay," He said, hugging me as tight as he could.

My face squished into his chest, I collapsed.

"Z-Zamirrldudittttt," I sloppily put together through heavy heaves and watery snot that ran amongst the outline of my cupid's bow. Six milligrams of salt sufficed, succeeding, releasing the gritty triumph of fighting tooth and nail for a Bachelor of Arts.

"We knew you would," He said over my loud cries, kissing my feverish forehead over and over again. "I'm so proud of you."

We were each other's standing support as I sobbed four years' worth of emotional labor for two hours straight. I put together small epiphanies and topped them with "And I did it, Z." Gallons of tears, snot and hot, reactive sweat rushed right out. Thank God he wore his rain jacket.

By 5:27 a.m., Zamir left me in my empty room to take a nap on my naked queen-sized mattress. Around 8:30 I got up, salty tears still sizzling on my tongue, still woozy from all the leucine enkephalin, but all packed up. I arrived to Maryland, face buttery and smooth after an organic face wash of tears in my most successful episode of human, emotional release.

I arrived cleansed.

about grief

Nicole Morris

it's not like Mister Green said it would be,
there is no la-la-la-la-ing your way free;
the trick to shaking off that dead weight,
of climbing outta that sinkhole of grief is this:
>   You gotta get yourself deep
>   into the woods/the dark
>   the green, the grass
>   into the moss, where coyote trails fade and
>   footpaths give way to shadows and gray,
>   where the air feels like high tide and begins
>   to take on a scent: wild and wet, cedar with clay, ash,
>   badger, flesh of aspen, river raw

Go there and get on your knees my darling—
No, not to pray, not to weep, but to reach
your fingers into the soil and pull out its soul,
Burrow deep enough to feel that hot sun-soaked top layer
give way to the cool wormy womb where
there has never been light:
>   enter that space, my child, put your mouth to that honey pot
>   and blow; let loose your pain; give to that space your keening,
>   your grief, your sorrowful sopping wet sad
>   that you cannot carry any longer.
>   leave it with them, the under-earth ones,
>   the they that have the strength to hold it
>   long enough to let it be water and food for bark,
>   twig, root, and eventually tree,
>   then oxygen that you, my sweet one, might breathe

godspeed, glore

Jasmine Knowles

This grief ain't nothing new,
This grief ain't nothing new,
This grief ain't nothing new,

> *Feet don't fail me. fathered heaven*
From down here
> > *fathered heaven*
> > *fathered heaven.*

From down here,

this body is a temple of memoirs never cracked
open of *my mother and my mothers mother and her mother
too*

Sometimes I just want
to write about love
But I am too tired.

Revolutionaries I can't trust

Brandy Collins

I can't trust a person who calls themselves a revolutionary and they don't do a little dance when a delicious plate of food is set in front of them.

I can't trust people who say "they never want to tell our stories" but don't read anything more than a meme or half a caption on some social feeds.

And what kind of worldly warrior are you when you drop swisher wrappers on the ground in the front of the store?

You ever meet a person who talks this talk about war and taking up arms and is ready to fight for freedom and ready to blow it up and ready to die? Now ask that same person what power looks like. What does it feel like? What does it smell like?

They won't have an answer; just repeating a problem they don't even fully grasp.

I can't trust someone who calls themselves a revolutionary who doesn't laugh out loud. What do you mean 'ain't nothing funny"? Everything is hilarious. Why aren't you fighting for the freedom to have joy and laugh and frolic?

I can't trust someone who calls themselves a revolutionary that tramples through a garden that isn't a part of the battlefield. Those roses that you are pulling from the stem for your amusement and lack of comprehension don't need you bleeding your traumatized recollection of survival on them. That softness and the delicateness are what this battle is for.

I can't trust a revolutionary who can't slow dance with a bottle of red wine after a long day of being a revolutionary.

I can't trust a revolutionary who can't see change when change is happening because in this battle they would never make it.

I'm thinking we are not fighting the same fight. I'm not fighting this fight to keep fighting. And yes, I said frolic and joy and delicate and freedom. Because the revolutionary I can trust understands those things.

No Poems Today

Aáron Breanna Heard

When reality becomes too much
To bear
Too heavy to hold
Too much to witness
Too much to transcribe
The poet
Leaves
The pen next to the paper
On the desk
Leaves
The space between the lines
Open
Leaves
The silence
To be heard
Loud and clear

How to Learn the Wrong Way to Grieve

Maya Williams

Accompany your Grandma Reece, your aunt, your uncle, and your siblings, to
      your PaRich's
plot. Arrange the fake red flowers in a vase with the knowledge of how your

grandmother will still want to exchange them seasonally for brand new pink
      plastic flowers.
While on your knees, to pray to give your PaRich some release, don't

argue with your grandmother as she forces you up by your elbow and drags you
      to her
car. Listen to her as she shouts, *Stop that. It won't bring him back.* Let her finish

her arrangements. Let Uncle Ricky and Aunt Karen continue
to say nothing. Let all your three siblings continue to say nothing.

Let yourself dust off the dirt from your knees. Learn to never
do that ever again as you visit PaRich's grave every year.

Don't let her know you already know he's not coming back.
Don't let her know that all you wanted was to cry it out. Don't

let her know that you wished everyone would cry along with you.
Know that when you bring this to her attention when you're old enough

and brave enough to do so, she'll widen her stare at you,
say, ... *Oh, I don't even remember that.* Keep your tears in.

My Dad is waiting to welcome me

Loraine Masiya Mponela

My Dad is waiting to welcome me
Early in life I had a lesson
Death came into my family
And reminded us of it's close
Proximity to humankind
Can't be resisted, dodged or postponed.

My dad's life
as cut short I was left orphaned
And now dad rests
in divine power
and eternally in our fathers kingdom.

I know my father
He waits for me in heaven
With his long warm hands
And tears in his eyes
Pre-cursing a flood of joy of our meeting

His calming smile shall welcome me
Our love will shine
We shall Hold hands in an eternal embrace
never to be Separated
Even for a moment

A Womb Story

Sherniece Johnson Smith

She never had a name. I never thought of "her"
I only thought about the consequences of her state of being:
>Bleeding or Not
>Cramping or Not
>Pregnant or Not...
She never had an identity of her own. Not until she was gone, my uterus.
I can recount the stories of the fibroids. How they affected my life, my
pregnancies, and my blood count.

I am saddened that my womb remained anonymous for all of
her life. Today, I will speak of her triumphs and accomplishments. I will
acknowledge her, her story will be told. My womb story begins during the
fall of our 13th year. We were in the 8th grade. It was a Sunday morning. I
felt a little sick, went to the bathroom and there was blood on the tissue.
I WAS A WOMAN! I GOT MY PERIOD!
I told my mom, she gave me some supplies – some of y'all might
remember the thick Kotex pads that had to be pinned to your panties. She
gave me instructions about how to take care of myself, and told me to come
to her if I had any more questions.
I also remember hearing my mom tell someone on the phone
"Lord, I hope she don't go and get herself pregnant".
Now I was scared of my period, my womb, and my womanliness...
"Pregnant" was a bad word in our house. The only pregnant people I had
been around were my cousins who were too young, too fast, no one was
happy about their pregnancies. I had a calendar that had puppies on the
cover; you know the ones the size of a checkbook. My mom told me my
period would come about every 28 days and that I had to keep track. I also
had to circle the actual day that it came on the Black History funeral home
calendar in the kitchen, the one with the doctor's appointments, bill due
dates and exterminator visits. (It wasn't until later that I figured out why).
My periods were pretty uneventful; they came and went quietly. I never had
cramps. I often forgot it was time for it, so I always carried supplies – just in
case.
I started having sex, went to the gynecologist for birth control and
when she felt around up there, I finally became aware of where my womb
was. I got my first look at her when the doctor felt fibroids and ordered
a sonogram. This was when the fibroids took center stage. The only time
my womb was mentioned was when we spoke about them. They were
in the walls of the UTERUS, at the back of the UTERUS, causing the

UTERUS to tip. They were affecting the lining and causing endometriosis. They would need to be removed. The UTERUS would be taken out, fibroids removed and Uterus replaced. We only spoke of her in "clinical conversations."

She came through the surgery like a Warrior Queen. She was scarred, but it did not change who she was. My periods were still unremarkable,

no cramps,

every 28 days,

like clockwork over in about 3 days – MY GIRL!

During the summer of 1995, my period did not come as scheduled; this was the first time in 15 years.

I was pregnant.

OMG! I had "gone and gotten myself pregnant" at 28. I was scared to tell my parents. It didn't matter that I had a college degree, a home and 2 cars, all in my name. It didn't matter that the baby's daddy was my high school sweetheart who also had a college degree and a "Good Job"! WE told them, I made him go with me so that they wouldn't act-up. They were OK, I wouldn't say happy, but OK.

On March 12, 1996, I started having contractions; I thought it was gas, because I had never really experienced cramps. I did not know that my UTERUS was flexing her muscles and preparing to release our daughter into the world. I quickly grew to know her power. This pain was something fierce. It took me out of myself, brought me to my knees and made me demand silence in the room from the beginning to the end of a contraction. This chick was a gangster!

Something went wrong, the baby's heartbeat dropped and we had to have an emergency C-section. She would be split open and stitched back together again.

TRAUMATIZED: she had cradled and nurtured her jewel to maturity, she was about to deliver her prize to the world, then all of a sudden: she was drugged, cut and her treasure stolen. Lastly, she was stuffed back into a space she had outgrown. It took some time, about three or four months for her to gather herself and get back on task. She didn't stumble. Every 28 days for 3 days. Over the years, the fibroids came back with a vengeance. We changed our diet, took both Western and Holistic, and more surgery.

My husband and I wanted more children, she would not hear of it. We accepted the fact that we would be a family of 3 and we were grateful for our daughter. It would be 10 years before she allowed another pregnancy. This time I had a period for the first 3 months, irregular but a period. I now wonder if she was still making up her mind, unsure if she wanted to try this again. During our first sonogram it was noted that the placenta covered the cervix. You see she had been so scarred that the most valuable of her real estate could no longer sustain life. We were told early on that this pregnancy would be ended 4 weeks early in an effort to prevent labor which would likely result in life-threatening blood loss. She would prepare to deliver her treasure for 8 months and then again it would be stolen. She would be drugged, cut then stuffed back into her holding place. It was December 7, 2006 – 65 years to the day after the attack on Pearl Harbor. Our condition was worse than anticipated. The fibroids had grown with our baby. The doctor made the standard bikini cut; the fibroids blocked the baby. The doctor then made a vertical cut; still she could not get to our baby. There we were crosscut, six fibroids were cut away so that our daughter could be freed. We were stitched up and she was returned to her place. We needed seven pints of blood; we had started the day with eight. This would be our last child; we had decided to have my tubes tied. We, neither she nor I could survive another pregnancy.

That spring she resumed her cycle; this time there was no rhyme, no reason. Calendars, comfort and control were all thrown to the wind. I would bleed when she said, for as long as she said, sometimes only a little, most times there would be flash floods. My Warrior Queen would have tantrums; she was scarred, angry and anything but steady. I had hoped that she would get her rhythm back; I prayed that everything would return to normal.

Two years passed, and I was getting weaker. My mother and other women were telling me to "get rid of that thing, you don't need it anymore, you have two kids and you won't miss your period". The doctors mentioned hysterectomy at every visit, it seemed they attributed all of my physical problems to monthly blood loss.

I did not want to have the surgery; I did not want to lose her. She had held and nurtured my beautiful daughters; she had provided an on-time and loyal service for 25 years. I felt like I had used her and was casting her away when she needed me most. On the other hand, she wasn't giving me anything to work with; the blood loss was killing me physically, I was weak, anemic, and mean. My quality of life was suffering; it had come down to her or me.

On October 3, 2012 I had a hysterectomy. The night before surgery, I apologized to her for what was to be done, I thanked her for all she had given. I prayed for her. I miss her; there is warmth where she used to be. I can still feel her Love, Power, Strength and Steadfastness. Even though there is no longer blood, I am still aware of my cycle. I pray that her transition was swift and that our journeys will continue to be blessed with Love and Light.

Let love

Daad Sharfi

> "let the war be won
> let love be
> at the end"
> —Lucille Clifton (Let there be new flowering)

Let love be
clarity
soft skin &
silk fingertips
wiping the crust off my eyes
Let it be a window facing northeast
speckled with your dirt & my dust
Let love wake me up just
in time,
as a slice of white light
cleaves day from night
Let love be cheek to cheek conversations,
let it age against its own reflection
Let love be
leaving
& looking back
Let love
let me see
love as sanctuary
love as safety
how trusting palms
will speak to each other
in the dark.

Memory

Kimani Rose

when the breath is lost
and the sinking continues
the deepening stays

does the water heal as well as I was taught?
or did this loss leave behind a betrayal
       the water doesn't heal
       the stars don't twinkle
       the joy has left my life
       the ears aren't perking up at the sounds of tortillas browned on the stove
       the hallways are no longer lined with photographs
       the couches aren't stacked in stuffed bears and dolls
       the air is cold year round

a grief sized hole through the center of chests
pendulums just to remind you- it hurts
       to know
       to remember
       to realize
       they're still gone after a deep breath

and in remembering- your breath is gone too

defeat your vanity

Raina J. León

vestige of when you wanted to be a nun,
charted your sins
tracked the ways of becoming
more saintly. you know that this is a lie,
too aware of how wildness is seen
in the mirror of the eyes around you.
you do not want to filter the gaze
of others into how you view yourself.
it is enough just to stay alive,
rather than constantly
deciphering how you are perceived
as living.

fly girl

Karla Tiffany

deep in swampbelly i seen mama
the conjurer wadin' in roux, thickenin'
souls swirlin' sol burnin' soles achin'
so i say
i wanna fly

and she turned
on me in cackles

she say
bring me the sweat
of the moon
as it tills
the fallen

her smile
a constellation
of wayward girls
seeking wings
to fly flyaway
like blackbirds
forged by fire

in his eyes
i stick to corners

and bottle the moonlight
as hair

in dandelion
fallin' in seams
of gumbo mama
conjures at new year
to ward off stench
of men she say
click your tongue three times

and slip out
in mornin'

so i leave broken
glass under window
and wait for my soul
to thicken
the ache
for a home
without walls
where i wade
in swamp water
conjurin' wings
for girls
on their way
to bed an
empty stomach
simmerin
in slurry
for girls
who ask
seconds
of a bare
pot in hand
shadows
beckonin'

a new me
to take flight

on the topic of:

Ayodele Nzinga

strong resilient black
women
when you
tell a black woman
she is resilient
you mean
she endured
some horrific
occurrence
& survived –
you aint said
nuthin
bout the cost of survival
or
estimated
how many demons
are hiding
in how many
sets of russian
nesting dolls
when
you say
to her
she's strong
what you mean
is –
yo' ass aint gone
crazy
yet?
what you miss
is
the way the
head still tilt toward sun
even with a face full of tears
how she go
forward
when
her feet can't touch

the ground
no more
she could tell you
it can cut you bad
this
going on
but tomorrow is
a place that might
hold her song
so she
go on
it's
whole-damn-ocean-ness
but
you got to have the word
for that
like
but-for-godz&sky-ness
she keeps unfolding
& you
wonder how she
hold all she
holding
bottomless
infinite
just call it
what it
is
nature-of-the-goddess
or
stand blindly
in its warmth & flow
until it
explodes

Peach River Prayer

Kenia D. Hale

Of course it was peach gum. The River could recognize the smell anywhere, and gurgled jealously, having tasted nothing of the flavor before but discarded pits and over ripe peaches heavy with worms that had dropped into its depths. It slowed and stilled as it felt the girls approach, their soft footsteps reverberating through the soil along the river bank. The girls came and sat, blowing peach flavored bubbles and picking at the muddy red clay as they talked with voices lightened in mid-afternoon Georgia sun. The River kissed their feet as they giggled by its edges, careful not to rush too fast as to wash them away. The River was heavy with Black bodies and sorrow, and wanted no more, longed for nothing more than to return the now River spirits to the Black lives they'd once been.

The water rippled with tadpoles and the girls' secrets. The River had always had a special place for these girls, girls who brought it sweet offerings of candy and flowers. These sweet girls, with voices that made the fish rushing by slow down to listen, hushed voices that tickled the lily pads and worms. Voices that kept even the mosquitos at bay. Here they were, sitting together under the old oak tree.

The River hurried the other creatures along with its waves, desired nothing more than to relish alone in the secrets of its favorite pilgrims. The girl with braids whispered of the passing of a favored Aunt, while the one whose hair reached towards the sun held her and caught her tears with her thumbs. The creatures around them grew hushed, and the River slowed in reverence. It remembered the woman. It had always recognized her presence, because she walked with a certain lightness. It was she who'd first brought the girl to its waters.

Back then, the girl was smaller, all beaded braids and scabby knees kissed with cocoa butter. Back when everything was new. The River had watched as this little girl scaled trees and sang songs to the branches, dug in the dirt with wooden kitchen spoons till she touched clay, hobbled along behind her mother in the garden in search of strawberries. Yet she never wanted to venture close to its waters. The River was curious, but knew better than to coax children to its depths.

The River remembered the Aunt's first visit, that lightness, watched as the girl tugged at the woman's long patterned skirts to be picked up. The laughter that spilled from the windows of the girl's home whenever the aunt was near, the smell of cornbread and greens so heavenly that the birds paused their song out of reverence. It was this aunt that first carried the little girl to the River side, coaxed her to touch the water while the girl's arms, still chubby with baby fat, clung around the woman's neck and cowrie shell necklace in fear. The girl had always taken after her aunt, sharing a skin tone dark and velvety as the soil in her mother's garden. The woman and girl sat next to the River that day, the first visitors that came simply to sit with the River, not to venture over it or dump trash into it or forage in its depths. The river found itself unsure of what to do and waited in anticipation while its guests basked in the Georgia heat. The aunt didn't rush the girl, simply sang prayers to the River while the girl stared at her, dark brown eyes wide with wonder. While her aunt sang, the girl slowly inched closer, then close enough to look over the edge at her own reflection. As the River gazed back at the girl, it saw in her eyes a curiosity and softness it hadn't felt in a long time. That day, seeing its reflection in the girl's eyes, the River learned to see itself anew.

That day, the aunt taught the girl that the water could be a confidant and friend, as long as she slowed down enough to hear its lapping waves. Over the years, the girl and the River developed certain understanding – the girl came to the River with her secret laughter and sorrow, and the River would hold them in its belly for safekeeping. In return, the girl would visit the River like a pilgrim, sit with it in the dusk while they both drank in the moonlight. Though her aunt lived by the sea, she would teach the girl new prayers and songs whenever she came to visit. The girl's aunt always greeted the river during her visits, and the two would sit at the water's edge as the woman taught the girl hushed water rituals. The River was always in awe of this alchemist from the sea, who taught her niece to place water under her bed to protect against nightmares and leave marigold petals by the River for the spirits in its depths. And always, always honeyed words and burning incense reserved for the water itself, as a protector of life and their people.

As the girl grew taller, she was careful never to bring anyone untrustworthy to the River's banks. When she had friends from school over, they skipped doubledutch in the front yard or gossiped near the old oak tree. But never close enough to disrupt the clay on the riverside, never close enough to hear the frogs croak during sunset. This place was reserved for the girl, her River, and her aunt.

Therefore, when the girl first showed up with her friend, the River knew this new girl must be special. And she was – the girl with the hair that reached for the sun gazed at the river with the same loving eyes as she stared at the River's beloved devotee. She joined their church easily, sat in nervous eagerness while the girl's aunt taught them to identify edible plants in the backyard and ancient dances to bring the rain. It was by the River that the girls practiced prayers and incantations that the aunt taught them, their giggles making the humid heaviness that much more bearable. It was by the

River that the girls shared their first secret kiss, parted lips sweet and sticky with summertime peaches. Later, it was by the River that the girls confided in the aunt about their shared feelings. The woman couldn't contain her excitement. Her joyful dancing reverberated through the ground against the River, her skirts flying as if, despite the lack of any kind of wind in the Georgia heat, she'd simply decided to create her own.

The River, a body filled to the brim with water, couldn't cry per se. But it felt so moved by the news of the aunt's passing. This aunt, who'd stored her prayers in the River's depths for safe keeping, prayers for her niece and the River and her family and her people. Who would never again recite her incantations or count her cowrie shells in the sun. The River felt itself rising in emotion, and it began to rush with rage at the thought of another beautiful Black life lost. It was tired of loss, tired of ruin. The tadpoles and fish and rocks were pushed downstream, frogs jumping to the banks to avoid the River's anger. The girls too, jumped back in surprise at the River's sudden fury. The River rarely showed this part of its power. It even contained itself during storms so as to avoid flooding the girl's nearby house, controlled itself to keep from hurting more people than it already had. But now, it heaved itself at the world with abandon and sorrow, lost in its grief for one who it knew so intimately.

The teary-eyed girl stared from the river bank in wonder. The same wonder from all those years ago. She'd never seen her confidant so upset, and didn't know what to do. More than anytime before, her heart ached for her Aunt, and her tears began to fall as fast as the river rushed. Her friend tentatively grabbed her hand and whispered to her, lifting her voice over the sound of the River's rush. She wiped away her friend's tears and held her close. Then the girls, locking eyes, stood up and started singing. They sang same secret prayers that the aunt had sang to the River all those times before. The River felt the vibrations of their clear notes over the sound of its own sorrow, and began to slow as to better hear their song.

From a distance, a woman in long skirts watched the young women hold each other and kiss tears from each other's cheeks. They paused for a moment to listen to the sound of the calming water. Then the pair laid out a blanket on the soft earth and opened the picnic basket they'd packed together. They laid out their spread – corn bread, collard greens, sweet potatoes and tilapia, with fresh sliced peaches and cream for dessert. Before they feasted, they grabbed one more thing from the basket – a bouquet of marigolds, fresh picked and still smelling of dew. The young women took turns putting a flower in each other's hair, giggling when they wouldn't sit straight but happy regardless. Then they went to the River and threw the rest of the petals in, the bright orange covering the water like rainfall. They even threw in some peach slices for added sweetness, then sat down to enjoy their feast. The woman behind the old oak tree watched as the water lapped happily at the young women's' feet, thankful for the color and the sweetness. Then the river stilled, as if recognizing familiar lightened footsteps barely kissing the ground. The woman smiled, content that all was as it should be. Then a rare Georgia breeze blew past, taking the woman and her skirts away with it.

Your Queendom Calls

dr. adrienne danyelle oliver

hey sis,

this is just a line to let you know that God see ya
the tears and the pain are
the rain
he sent to free ya
the world see your strength
and they always
wanna be ya
Diva
you the meaning of
the universe
being so Divine
been a blessin
   and a curse
always tryna steel ya light
because you got the most
shine
always tryna make you late
when you on Divine time

This is a just a line to let you know
to keep goin
never play it small
because you got a big showin
                  flowin
your rhythm is
the beat of nation
without your womb
there would be
   absolutely no creation
Haitian
   like a revolution
let your Spirit rise
commanding all shadows
to bow to the light
the Queen has arrived
and she's

the coldest winter ever
the mind of her spirit
turn a brick into a feather
coal becomes gold in the presence
of her light
surrender to her
alchemy
and getcha mind right

This is just a line, sis
to remind you of your purpose
the pain and the tears are part
of dress rehearsal
it's showtime now
Apollo
   you got wings
time to take flight
and handle Queen tings

love always,
Your Inner Queen

Metta to Our Healing

Sarai Bordeaux

Remembering how inherently worthy we are,
Sending Metta to the times we forget.
Holding our bodies in hopes of health,
Sending metta to the times when there was no care.
May we be kind to ourselves,
May we take time to become as full as the moon.
May we stop everything to indulge in the deepest breath.
May we wonder and run from waves on the beach like children.
May we protect the water.
May we not fear our feelings.
Sending Metta to each time we've allowed ourselves to break
down. Metta to the process of breaking down.
To the way nature plays with us.
To the giggles of the Universe.
Metta to the ways that love drags us sometimes.
To the ways that acting in love is hard.
To the ways we get when we know things are not ok.
Metta to not being ok.
Sending Metta to ourselves and our spirits and our bodies.
To finding and allowing for homes to form within our bodies with safety and
acceptance. Metta to the ways we have been unskillful.
Metta for the allowance of healing
Metta to the peeling.
May we seek to uncover more
Metta to all animals, to all living beings.
Metta to the things that make it possible for us to live.
To the things that make life better.
May we care for each other more.
May we learn from each other more.
May our instincts deepen to heal our lands.
Sending Metta to the spaces within which we seek courage
Metta to the space where we have not been courageous yet.
Sending Metta to our food choices,
To all of our choices.
May we nourish ourselves and find recourse within each.
Remembering that sometimes choices have not been ours to
make. Some choices are still not ours to make.
May we still act freely.

Metta to the ways we seek comfort.
May we continuously feel into our cycles.
Sending Loving Kindness to the ways we need these cycles.
To the ways we brood and shed.
Sending Metta to the ways we have not held ours and others suffering
skillfully. To the ways we still do not know the impact of our egos.
May we be healed in the lessons that need repeating.
May we not fear repetition.
May we not fear the shaking of our voices,
The tears in our eyes
Or the tremble in our feet moving forward.
Metta to the moments we are sure liberation exists
And to the times we are still uncertain and tired of waiting.
May we move toward our freedom
Always.
Sending Loving Kindness to all aspects or our every selves.
In Gratitude
In Remembrance
Asé

Metta is a Pali word signifying the expression of loving-kindness toward all beings
including ourselves. The cultivation and practice of Metta has significant importance
within a Buddhist context and can be exercised through meditation among other
ways. This Metta was written by Sarai Bordeaux to accompany a group meditation
with the BIPOC Sangha hosted by Dhamma Dena Meditation Center on Serrano,
Chemehuevi, and Cahuilla land, also known as Joshua Tree, California.

Checkmate

Felicia Johnson

a tisket, a tasket
my hips resemble a basket
full and swaying
treasured and praised
carrying memories of
the ages
remembering the future pages
books untold
letting wealth unfold
praying over spirits unsold
oldest nights
elder thoughts and whispers
berry-filled branches with roots deeper
than you can see
the sea bleeds with the visions
time reads the mysteries
the waves tell stories of the bones underneath
ruby-laden, gold-weighted freedom
they sought it
the ocean holds secrets well
holds more than it can tell
but it comes out in the prayers
in the napes of necks
with grandaddy's eyes
and aunt mary's name
in that old spirit
with all new parts...

I dare you

Alie Jones

*Black women make up 40%
of humans being trafficked
in the United States*

I dare you
to SEE Black girls
Witness the almond-colored
triumph in our eyes
To recognize Black girls
Beyond the colonizer lies
I dare you to release instant gratification/ exploitation

Our pain cannot be fixed with a bandaid
Black girls are not a gas station or shopping mall
We are short and fat and thin and tall
Wilting and blooming
So much more than the eye can see
We wear crowns that get heavy

I dare you to HOLD SPACE
for Black girls who
bloom in a drought
Black girls who
ask too many questions and
don't learn from our mistakes
From the sweetest sunflower to
the thorniest rose

I dare you to
EMBRACE Black girls
Falling apart in front of you
Who are too loud, too fast, and have an attitude
Black girls with beads and barrettes
With scars, we can't forget

I dare you to be courageous
To stand up and
LOVE Black girls
Who could use a hug or two

Deserving of care and adoration
Momma, Mentor, Auntie;
Nurture the mending.
You are a mirror of joy and affection

Granny, Teacher, Sister;
I dare you to stop saying this ain't
your problem
Stand up and fight
Be the glimmer of light

I dare you to PROTECT Black girls
Shine Brighter than the storms you've faced
To be a lighthouse when fog rolls your way
To move with deliberation and grace.

Sag Cider

Raheem Divine

Fire Cider is a blend of spices, herbs, roots, and other natural ingredients that aid in boosting immunity and overall health. This tonic has been known to ward off the cold and flu, ease sinus congestion, and improve digestion. The following recipe is my own rendition of the cider that I call "Sag Cider". The name was inspired by my Sagittarius sun sign and honors the healing power of fire energy.

Ingredients:
Apple Cider Vinegar
Echinacea
Eucalyptus
Oregano
Sage
Thyme
Ginger Root
Turmeric
Lemons
Oranges
Onions
Garlic
Peppers of choice
Horseradish
Honey
Instructions:

Add ingredients to a glass jar. Store in a dark, cool place. Brew for at least 4 weeks. Shake occasionally. Strain liquid & Enjoy!

Tip: Dilute before use.

You can consume with water, add to tea, add to soup, use as marinade, or use as salad dressing.

My Kind

M. Nzadi Keita

Some words came raining.

If those words were spoken with a bemused smile, or even as a friendly tease, once in a while, I could've shaken them off. But in the world outside of books, this view was common. Peevishly and frequently expressed – whether in actual word darts or blunt-tipped shrugs, I caught an attitude: side-eyed and mystified, stiff lips stuffed with downcast judgements, dissatisfied, slow-swung heads.

If all that rain of harsh talk and hissing was supposed to stop me, well. Too bad. It did just the opposite. When I got old enough to walk more than a block alone, I did. One right turn at the end of the street, up the long hilly sidewalk, and beyond two easily-crossed streets, there Lovett Library sat, waiting. The door pulled open to that dove-grey glass house, stacked high with words.

I would dive, kicking, gliding down into pages, deaf to opinions. Going places. I found words could be tickets to travel. Umbrellas against the rain that sometimes crystallized to hail.

I had a cousin who could tolerate me. We were word nerds of different sorts, although both entranced by the idea of mail. A goofy, mundane correspondence bounced us both through puberty. Diaries and mental lists kept us afloat when pleasure-reading time shrunk.

College. No one around me had enough experience, if any, to say much. Good choices, bad choices, unidentified traps or shining pathways, they would be all mine to suss. They figured I would figure it all out. Always reading something anyway. Right?

I was going to be a writer, I said. Unaware, then, of how the world smirked a bit at such a notion: some un-moneyed, unspectacular Black girl. Where was there to go with that fixation but out? Daring myself, I had launched into a new city, onto a large campus, into strange surroundings, accents, climates, and assumptions. I stumbled into a small, quirky circle, a gang of women. With them as affirmation, I seemed to shave the edges off of that daunting leap.

Words were what I could handle; they had carried me that far. So I was going to be a writer, period. Unaware of what such a claim brought with it: a level of alone that would spiral me back home, to another, larger school, with cheaper in-state tuition. Alone in class, at the subway, on the bus. With no gang, no cushion of laughter, the silences went long. Too long, sometimes, but I chose this road.

Hadn't words always made me a loner? Alone could seem like the quiet of a door, gently closed against arrows of doubt, but was the knob now quietly locking?

A plain blue book from the library, The Four-Chambered Heart, had snagged my eye. Like fish in a net, the title somehow drew me. I poured it down like a drunk on a bender the first time, done in two nights. I read it twice. Words that mopped up my cracked, leaking mind. Words that took a newspaper to my fogged inner mirrors. Words that wrapped me in gauze. They sealed off the arrow dents and divots from the comments landing on my essays for school.

Who wrote that thing? Anais Nin. Some French woman. Or French-speaking Spaniard. A complicated European who had lived in 1930s France. Ran with an artsy crowd. Overdosed on Henry Miller and fled World War 2 for the U.S. Sex slinked in the crevices between lines, in the doubled spaces.

I overdosed on her words, reading every volume of the diaries she published. I had to tell her. If she was still alive, I had to tell how her words took me in when doors kept shutting as soon as I stepped forward. If anything followed the silences, it would be arrows of rain, and yet, her words had created a place, dry and sunny, that affirmed me: oddity of a Black girl, born to do this thing.

August, 1976. Alone in the little apartment where I staked my declaration of independence. Sitting between two box fans, sweating delirium, I scrubbed a line of dirt that, I discovered, had been painted into the woodwork. A break became irresistible.

What fun to try the mailbox key, I thought. In those days before junk mail, all that came was all there was. No California postmark made sense. The Scripps-Howard fellowship had sent its thin envelope, their 'no thank you.' No one in Los Angeles knew me. Who could have sent an envelope that started there, stamped with a unique fish logo, bearing that exceptional font, a box number, and incredibly, the name above it? Anais Nin.

What did I write, out of isolation and painful need? Why did I think of it? Maybe after the major magazine I pitched to stole my idea and sent a ten-dollar check. Maybe once I signed the lease and stood in the sunny front room of that apartment, feeling bold. I had found the address for her publishing company, and stayed up late, spilling words. I had virtually put a message in a bottle, carried out on a sea of air.

"I admire how your mind has found its way to a different inner life. I have been fighting cancer for 2 years and my energy is so low that I have to reduce my correspondence and visits, but I could not leave your sincere and feeling letter."

Anais Nin wrote back. She mentioned James Baldwin and Canada Lee.

She wished me happiness. A precious batch of words from a writer who would be dead five months later, turned me toward the practice of writing to writers. A healing certainty came that I was right in choosing what chose me. Out of bright glad shards, out of boundless frustration, with or without a reply, I would continue from then on, making bridges out of words to seek out my kind.

By Breath or By Prayer

Yeva Johnson

With a breath and my feet
Anchored to earth
I travel out, in, or deep
The essence of me touches
The essence of a being
Alive or not, on earth or not
With my feet on earth
My breath buoys me &
In a flash I am right
Where I need to be

Grief Meditation (Double Sonku)

Julia Mallory

I'm sending
my grief through
the soles of
my feet. Through
to the earth
that's ancient.
Through to the
earth that is
perfectly
formed. Through to
the earth that
can hold it.

ANCESTOR

Natachi Mez

I asked your name
You told me anytime I
exhale It is as if I am
calling you
And with each inhale
You are responding
I gasp and we know
That lineage is not linear
what has died touches the
living You touch me
Transform me
Unformed and now I am
Root and stem and blossom and
fruit all at once
I am growing and harvested
A bountiful death

You said I love you
It is baptism
A mirror, we reflect each other
Take me in
To our completion
There are no differences between our
names Time collapses between us now
I love you and now love myself
I call you and you
Are me, weapons formed
against us Molded into
ego-death
Scattered development
Exposed, light on film
Shuttering, shuttering into
Immortal baptism

PART II:
INTIMACY GRIEF REST

Kaleidoscope

Sonia Sanchez, Homegirls & Handgrenades

tumbling blue and brown
tulips that leap
into frogs
women dancing in metal
blue raindrops sliding
into green diamonds
turtles crawling outward
into stars
spreading beyond words
papooses turning
into hearts
and butterflied stretching
into court jesters
who jump
amid red splinters
just like you.

THE DANDELION RITUAL

Lyn Patterson

for letting go of dreams
you are no longer manifesting

Need:

Blooming dandelions (the yellow ones) one per each dream you are releasing.

Full grown dandelions (the white ones) one per each new dream you plan to manifest.

Ritual:

Pick the yellow dandelions first. Acknowledge each thing you are letting go of, by saying it out loud. This signifies its importance and the necessity of mourning. Pick full grown dandelions from their root. As you determine each new dream, blow all the seeds, until there are none left. This symbolizes trust in the universe and willingness to allow its flow. Place all dandelions in a vase together on your altar, do not water, let nature take its course. This is a reminder of the cyclical nature of all things.

When You See a Black Woman Pass You on the Street

Kelechi Ubozoh

The sun and I
make direct
eye-contact
Her brilliance
doesn't scorch me.
We will warm each other.

THE MOTHER OF ALL JAMS

Tawhida Tanya Evanson

Even before we knew we were in the machine, it was a reckoning.
Hot air sucked you quick off the stack into a vortex shock on an obstacle
    course at high speed.
Parent and child in a fight. A micro war between us from the word no.
One criminal act gave way to conflict crash
And sixty-five hundred volts later we were machine and product, you and I
Unruly sheets bunched up, looped and curlicued round themself in the dark
Mummified because neither product nor machine would give an inch.
Someone used an air knife and we're down.
Mother and daughter cut down in the street or in a cage at the border we built.
Not all papers are created equal. Some are seized, some disappear.
Others generate friction, red tape, white flags light up as refugees travel the
    machine.
Pushed into the same space all at once. Kids jammed up. For months. Years.
    Underground even.
Papers become piles of non-linear petals dumped into one mass grave.
Each page. Different from the same. Hemp, straw, flax, rags, wood chips
    drenched in acid.
All take a soaking, a ferment, a beating before being reduced to fibers.
Pressed to a pulp and stuck in the mother of all paper jams: a flower
    arrangement.
A removal from home. Error. Terror inside the mother machine.
The heart itself, path-smart, knows the way. If we let it.
O drum assembly, bring our edges into alignment, guide us on through

That Special Recipe from Grandmothers and their Mothers Too

Yeva Johnson

With gratitude to Aurora

Ingredients:
  a big cup of Africa
  a jigger of Europe
  a pinch or a handful of Native America
  2 ways to answer the Bluest Eye and Yellowest Hair Questions
  A bowl that holds a 23-hour workday
  Thaw out 60 minutes of rest
  Knowledge of how to sew & a dozen ways to make bread rise
  Liberal quantities of the ability to keep secrets
  A dash of cut them with your eyes
  A lb. of premonitions of the future, set out to come to room temperature
  4 cups grated wisdom beyond your years

Directions:

Get your bowl ready on the countertop of life. You might not have all the ingredients yet, but just use what you've got and add the rest whenever it comes. Start with the big cup of Africa and slowly mix in that jigger of Europe and sprinkle the Native America all over. Mix well. Sew up clothes from scraps, and plenty of quilts from scraps, because it's not just food that keeps you warm. If time is running short, warm up the premonitions of the future in the microwave. Make cornbread, Johnny cake, pound cake, rolls, and biscuits, always enough to feed two or three more than you expected. Cradle your granddaughter's face in your hands as you share the two ways you can answer her Bluest Eye and Yellowest Hair questions so she can continue to grow, to know she is already somebody to love. Only share what and when the granddaughter needs to know it. Fold the rest of the secrets into the batter and then pour into a pan big enough for the world. Sprinkle liberally with grated wisdom and a dash of cut them with your eye. Put it all into the oven of creation. Let this epigenetic cake bake until it's sweet, spicy, rich aroma calls to all family past present and future. That's when you'll know it's ready and you can share a slice with everyone.

Enjoy: by eating your fill and putting your feet up for 60 minutes of rest and a chance to exhale

Serves: a whole family, every generation

Good Morning, Heartache

Danielle Mason

They make jokes about the strong Black woman, without really taking a moment to understand her pain. It is a revolutionary act to be soft during tumultuous times, but it is also very dangerous. A Black woman who presents herself as an I can do bad by myself type, taking on traits of masculinity is not a hater of men, she is tired. Her softness has taken on a form of protection in order to survive. Her mind is reclaiming its power to be sound and focused, healed and ready. I want so badly to be soft during these times, but society won't let me. My man won't let me. The second that I try to relax, I am being lazy. The minute that I ask for help, I am using someone. Taking care of the responsibility of tending to my children, couldn't possibly be deemed as work, because that's what I was created to do. I'm being asked to sacrifice myself for the common good, but really the good ain't that common.

I got a man but I'm stressed out about food. Because I get food stamps he doesn't feel responsible about whether or not his kids will eat. No matter how I attempt phrase my concerns, I am viewed as problematic because I am not willing to settle for less. People love to paint Black women as the enemy without realizing the burdens that we wear daily. I hold so much on my shoulders. I literally have knots on them from bearing all of the weight. We take on micro-aggressions from living in the white man's world, trying to get ahead while proving that we can stay true to our roots, and simultaneously carry Black men to let them know that we value their worth. But really Black men want to be white. They want a taste of the patriarchy— to reign supreme and to wreak havoc on those they deem as lesser beings.

If I'm not being soft enough, talking sweetly enough, smiling enough, or yielding enough...it's because I am tired. Not inconsiderate, not demeaning, but tired. The whole world feeds off Black women for our strength and tenacity, our ability to soothe and sustain, to endure and withstand, but the second she uses that energy to lift herself up, she's a bitch, she's selfish, she mad. Well, we've got the right to be mad. I told my daughter that sometimes it's okay to be angry and to cry. That those emotions have the power to connect you to your purpose and can drive action for good. So to keep it all the way real, fuck the patriarchy! Fuck trying to save face and keep it cute. Judge ya mama, not me. I will always stand up for what I believe and laugh in the face of danger. You've got me fucked up if you believe I will ever be complacent.

For the sake of the family, they say...you should suffer in silence. Get over yourself and sacrifice your ego. There are children involved. I sacrifice so much more than my ego for my children. I sacrifice my body, my time, my energy, my hopes, and my dreams. I sacrifice my expectations and my standards. The truth is that I need to have an ego when it comes to my children. I need to take a stand because the last thing they need to see their mother doing is suffering. My suffering affects them in ways you'd never imagine. They deserve my fullness.

I'm supposed to sit back and be quiet, keep it cute while a mother-fucker is disrespecting my womb. The very place that I opened up to him, he abuses the privilege. I can endure but only for so long, and only if it is working towards a common cause. I know how to coexist with him in a way that doesn't limit my capacity, but ultimately that means moving as if he is not there. I feel like if I have to pretend that a person is not there, in order for me to survive, then I might as well not have that person around at all.

He is a figment of my imagination.

What is it that makes me beg him to hear me when it's clear that he has his ears closed? I often think about his cognitive dissonance and the delusions he prioritizes over the truth, but then I am reminded of how the truth is subjective, and that maybe my perception of things is what causes me pain. I try to ignore him, to go on living and loving my babies despite his inability to show up for us, but his absence remains the big elephant in the room. I know what's behind the looks, given by my mom and my sisters, when I start to talk about doing this thing alone. They think it's a self-inflicted wound that has me pregnant and raising two little ones so far from home, without community, or even a dime of support from him.

Am I being delusional in having expectations? I mean who really would want to go through pregnancy alone? And even though I can find re-placements to fill the void left by him, they didn't create this baby. He asked for this. A family. To go half on a baby. He put it inside of me, and yet finds every reason to keep away. Mama's baby. Papa's maybe.

I really do try to have a normal conversation with him, to make small talk at times, but he equates the stress of having paint all over his body, to my swollen feet, anemia, and cramped stomach. I've got to keep my sights set on my blessings. I know they are here, I've just got to reach out and grab them. Honestly, if he were more transparent with me, I would be a bit more understanding, but I never signed up to be ignored. I didn't agree to move all the way across the country to be left abandoned. I moved here for him…with him, with our future in mind. But the only future I can see now is one of me taking care of these kids alone.

Spirit Break

Daya Stanley

Press tired bodies to pray bound hands to
systems no longer
sustained.

Find god in collards,
okra and cousin
Slyvia's last dollar.

Prayer cloth hid away For days when
bread could not stave Off the pain.
For nights when
the heat
being off disturbed
their slumber.

Meet saints on dark streets under liquor store marquee Down bottles find
the verses
Of hymns sung
At no choir rehearsal.

home is where the heart is

Mallessa James

Home is where the heart is.
This is a figurative statement about what it means to have a sense of
belonging, about how our understanding of our place in the world is
grounded by connections and
defined by relationships.
And yet your heart is literally in your body.

Which might suggest that your home is here within you.
That you are already and always at home.
Indeed, your body is the only home you will ever truly know,
the only home you can ever really call your own.
It's your 'forever' home.
Or perhaps until death do you part.

But let's be clear: you don't exactly own the place.
You are here because it pleases your body to have you here.
Because your body is willing to try to support you
and care for you while you hang around and do your thing.
It lets you think you're in charge because that's the easiest way to manage you.
But you belong here, in the strictest sense of the word.
You belong to your body.
It has you, you do not have it.
It's not like you have a choice.
You don't have someplace else to go.
You can't escape or run away and join the circus.
Because your mind is not like a software program that is simply running on
the hardware of your body.
You are not a ghost in a machine.
You are not somehow haunting your body.
Although it's quite possible that, technically, the sense of being you isn't even
        real. That it is
only a figment of your body's imagination.
That your body happens to have a brain that happens to create
patterns that happen to shape the perception of the you that you happen to
        believe yourself to be.
That your feelings and thoughts are really just your body talking to itself.
So even though your body is your one true home,
you are not actually a being that lives inside your body.

You are your body's inner experience of being alive.
Because to be alive is to be a body trying to
be at home within itself, in hopes of becoming a home who has learned to
create its own sense of
belonging.

Dream with me

Zhalisa Clarke

Close your eyes.

Dream with me.

I dream of a day when every breath feels *easy.*

I dream of a day when I can trust,
from the deepest part of my bones,
that the world is safe for people that look
like *me.*

I dream of a day when the wounds of my ancestors
finally complete their healing process,
ending generations of pain,
full stop.

I dream of a day when I look in the mirror and
see a reflection of beauty;
finally, truly, being able to see the
true me.

I dream of a day when I feel seen and heard
everywhere I go, and with anyone that I meet;
school, work, hospitals, stores,
everywhere.

I dream of a day when I feel loved for all of me;
for the naps in my hair and the sass in my smirk,
for the light in my soul, and the fire in my belly,
all of me.

I dream of a day when my weeks feel like
I'm floating in the calmest ocean; slow and easy,
rocked like a baby, back and forth and forth and back,
exhaling.

I dream of a day when I'm not afraid
to remove my armor,

piece by piece because…
no one's going to *hurt* me.

I dream of a day when my inhale is
slow and deep, and deep and slow.
I dream of a day when my exhale meets her
like the warmest of kisses, nourishing and *full*.

Dream with me.

Feel what this feels like with me:

like sunshine in the early morning, golden and glistening,
like the best hug you've ever had, filled with warmth and love,
like peace so deep it runs through every cell of every part of your body,
like fresh lemonade in the summer, and hot chocolate in the winter,
like you can

finally,

finally,

finally,

exhale.

Salt Water Mumbo Jumbo

by Karla Clark

you can feel it
in the water
the salt
the onion
the ham hocks

her hands
the garlic

her hands
smell like garlic
you can't feel
the heat
you grab mouthfuls
hoping to burn
her hands on
your tongue

at dinner
you serve prayer hands
empty chairs
her fingertips
cut across
your cheek and you

whisper garlic
her hands

simmer
reduce
reduce
until she can no longer
reach

reduces her hands smell
the smell of her hands her
hands smell like you
can't
feel
so you add garlic speak

garlic weep garlic to conjure
hands
that never taste
the same

stone throat

Raina J. León

something i want to say has created the rough. it is the size of an apple core, pebbled over like newly quarried granite encased in concrete that's been pitted by salt and weather through a hard winter. add in a thin layer of fiery that hisses each time i swallow.

my body tells me this. then i type technological prayers. *what does it mean, elder google?* it gives me images of the blue throat chakra, *vissudha*, in a language it does not identify, but i learn that in English it means, "pure" or "purification". I don't know what to take from elder google who is really my junior stuntin'.

the tapping of my keys is a rushed and stilted falling of water over smooth stones. if i just type the right prayer, i can at least smoothe the stone. i no longer hope to remove it so i can breathe. it has its own movement. i release ownership over it.

my lungs respond to the land with closer attunement each year. in summer 2020, as we in california feared the deepening drought and the fires it made more likely, my chest began to sputter with occasional sparks. first one fire, then another across northern california, then to the east and the south. eventually, so thick was the ash in the sky that it blocked out the sun in an orange haze. i never left the house. we ran air purifiers, with their low hum, throughout the day. our home became a bee hive in sound and motion. i walked the rooms carrying an air monitor and compared it to the air quality index. busy, busy, buzz. inside, i listened for the rustle of wind in the young lemon tree near the window where i nursed my daughter, only a few months old at the time. even in stillness, even rocking, buzz. there were no bees so we created the sounds of life.

my lungs began to get worse and worse. i couldn't breathe. i felt fatigued. the smallest actions made me tired. doctor after doctor. i bought enough supplies for my own medical office in my home. i thought it must be an anxiety attack extended since every test seemed to show me fine. everything was fine. fire all around and in.

peak flow meter. oximeter. blood pressure monitor. air quality monitor. eventually an emergency inhaler. and a regular inhaler. everything was fine.

at a conference during the height of the fires, after 15 minutes of sitting and watching the screen, the pulsing static in my chest rose quickly, taking my breath away. i had to sign off, lay down. i pulled out the peak flow meter and with all my strength blew. 68. normal is around 350 for my height and age. i put an oximeter on my finger. 91%. hovering. a dip. 90%. below 90 one is supposed to the hospital. i watched it hover, the over-achiever in me wanting it to rise. i fell asleep with the monitor in my hand.

outside the winds were still, the haze a caustic gaze barely shifting through the air. still with heightened senses so soon after birth, i could smell the slight charcoal grit even inside. sometimes i imagined breathing burned horses or owls or construction materials or all the other casualties of fire, which burns as it licks the land clean to black.

the doctors clearly thought my breathing was a mental condition as well ... until they saw the dual pleural effusions on my lungs. already the signs of damage, revealed in filmy white on black.

something i want to say is lodged in my throat. typing moves around the stone, a mounding deluge, to sweep the stone away.

i am not a being of fire. i am so much walking tinder. made for wet and earth and swallowing whole.

Moon Child

Raheem Divine

What do we do as a community when our babies don't wanna be here anymore?
Do we have a budget for this?
Can you point me to the line item?
How much funding do we need to keep our children here?
How do we measure the needs of a Moon Child?
How many board meetings will it take?
What's on the agenda?
Musk on the moon
Our babies leaving too
No aircraft though, just wings they grew when they decided that this life ain't
      what it do.
Heading to the moon in masses
If I send out this Zoom link will they still fly away?
Will Slack bring them back?
Ohhh, I got it. Crypto!
So how much will I need to save our kids tho?

They Were Right

Clinnesha D. Sibley

Our ancestors had it right.

Life is a continuum and we are visitors on this planet.

They knew we could not handle the ravages of this world in our own
strength, so they gave us

songs to sing if ever we were on the other side of the track, and it's dark, and
we are terrified.

They left us their hymns of hope, their battle cries, and their gems for

injustice. They taught us how to pray and not become prey.

How to intercede.

They gave God to us!
and helped us to see that the Holy of Holies was a state of being.

They told us to leave our burdens with the Lord and that we'd rest better if
we could just do that.

They taught us how to sacrifice a praise and they magnified Jesus so we
would come to know
real, sacrificial love.

Yes, our Grandmamas did that.

They gave us a plan for defense and a strategy for tragedy.

They knew that we alone were not equipped to handle these adversities,

the losses…

the suffering and emptiness…

They knew that grief was a continuous freight train
rushing across a steel railway in our backyard.

It screams at us and we scream back.

Our souls are crying out
     and we are a mess,
         muddling through our millennial minds,
            tripping over our words and woke-ness.
Our Mamas had it right.
They knew we had to be forgeable and tough, just like the steel.

And they were so right.

Without an ever-living One, our ancestors knew we'd become too paralyzed
     by death, forgetting
that it is indeed not permanent.

Before we knew the ancestral plane was real, our beautiful people gave us
     imagery of heavenly
gates and told us that one day we would see them all standing there with
     open arms…

I am convinced, though.

Paradise is an expansive field and our stories of joy and pain dwell in the
     skies above it.

And freedom…
     freedom is something they know,
         that we have yet to encounter.

Everybody's Voice Got a Little Something In It*

Julia Mallory

It's the grief itching
the back of my throat
How I grab this tired breath

Drag it through and
scratch what ain't got
a big enough name

I unchoke
And let a river cover me
or an ocean
A spoonful of water
can still drown you

What's the name of the
body of water
that took you

U

N

D

E

R

In my darkest days
my voice turned into
a hammer
in my sleep and
crushed my left molar
My jaw holding the weight
of my world

I learned to plant my tongue
against the roof of

my mouth
and let it fold into
the ridges of rugae
A reversal of gravity
I am upside down
in years
But not faith

I am not letting go

Twitter user May C. Black (alias)

"Lay all that mess down": A Story of Black Maternal Loss, Survival, & Liberation

Ebony Lumumba

For all the mamas holding their babies in their hearts.

The beeping made her nervous and she watched the bouncing green line on the monitor to distract herself from the warm liquid leaving her body. The nurse had asked her twice if she'd wanted to call someone to be with her—"the child's father maybe?" She could barely breathe let alone call someone. Besides, she needed to be alone with her body and whatever was happening inside it. Three times before she had flushed clumps of scarlet and purple down drains and watched them disappear. Choking her with grief. No one was there then. Why shouldn't she be alone now?

She had laid in that sterile room for two days ignoring the sounds her phone made—feeling ignored. The doctor had only come in once to say, "You've been through this before. It gets easier." What could be easy about life leaving your womb without your permission? His smugness made her hot. She bit the insides of her mouth when he began poking around inside of her with icy metal. She wanted to spit the metallic taste forming in her cheeks as he scribbled private notes about her private parts onto a chart she could not see.

The nurse moved around the room with no feeling—like she was not laying there open and holding her breath and gripping the rails of the bed with every piercing sensation. She closed her eyes and her mouth and tried not to breathe in the smell of the nurse's perfume. Flowers. Flowers were for marrying and dying. She wasn't doing either. So, she held her breath and tried not to be where she was. How could this woman do work in a room with so much sadness and not look at her eyes to make sure she wasn't dead. When the nurse left, she slowly pulled her body up and brought each of her legs to the left side of the bed. The beeping was so loud now. Her womb was so heavy. Stepping onto the cold floor with her bare feet felt like the first acknowledgment that she was alive. The floor responded to her swollen warmth unlike the nurses and assistants and the doctor who all looked at each other when they were supposed to be talking to her. The cool tile calmed the fire in her feet. She exhaled and whispered, "thank you."

Escaping the beeps and bouncing line was what she wanted. She yanked at the tubes keeping track of her body. They could have just asked her how she felt. Those machines didn't know. Her steps were slow. She imagined the floor was massaging the life back into her bulging feet and hissed small bursts of air as she stepped from white tile to black tile to white tile to black. Walking slowly to somewhere dark where there was air. Where she could sit with herself and weep for the child that wouldn't be. Unashamed of all the life leaving her. Not a bathroom. Her baby—the blood she always touched as it left her—wouldn't be mingled with the stuff that was supposed to leave her body this time. "Somewhere else." she thought. "There's gotta be somewhere else."

She pushed open a door that had no label. No sign of what it was or what was inside and found a small closet where the lady that came in her room early in the mornings kept her things. Miss Mary. That's who she said she was. She was the only one who asked her what her name was and what she liked to be called. "You want this window open, baby?" Miss Mary had made her feel soft like she did when she was a little girl as she moved around the room humming gospel songs and asking her where she wanted her water pitcher and extra towels. "Yes ma'am." "No ma'am." Was all she could muster to say as her insides throbbed and Miss Mary cleaned. She wanted her to stay. This gentle, sweet lady who gave her extra blankets and fussed under her breath that they hadn't let her soak her feet in some Epsom.

"Girl, your feet like to fall off if you don't get them down in some saltwater. Cain't believe they got you in here just a'hurtin' like this. Good for nothing."

Miss Mary's fussin' slowed down the beeping. She stopped holding her breath to breathe in the smell of castor oil and baby powder she brought into the room, and it lulled her to sleep. She cried when she woke up and saw Miss Mary was gone.

She sat in Miss Mary's closet touching the bottles and rags. Searching for her scent. This woman who had brought healing into her too cold, too sad room with her kind voice and tough, brown skin. There was a bucket turned over with a worn-out, home sewn pillow sitting on top. That had to be where Miss Mary sat when she wanted to get away from the beeping and the good for nothings.

She lowered her soreness onto Miss Mary's makeshift stool. Air left her mouth in a deep sigh. She picked up the book that sat next to a bottle of indistinct powder and opened it to the dogeared page. She read, "Lay all that mess down." Miss Mary had underlined it in red and circled it twice. The words of Baby Suggs, holy, echoed within her. "Lay all that mess down." When they'd told her she was due in August, she remembered that no one had ever call her "mama." The little lives that took over her womb always escaped before it was time. Left out of her body in viscous knots she knew were coming because of the pain—suffocating her with the knowing. "Lay all that mess down." Her chest heaved and tears raced down her face past her chin—saturating her thin hospital gown.

"It was time to lay it all down." Baby Suggs, holy, had said it.

That she could lay it down. Miss Mary had seen it and circled it in crimson. Lay it all down. Pass on the pull in her belly that made her stop every hour to cry because there would probably never be a baby. Lay it down.

Imagining she was in the Clearing with the laughing mothers, her air came in bursts. She covered her mouth with her hand to control her laughter. Rocking back and forth on Miss Mary's seat, she tapped her feet to the rhythm in her chest like that of a Djembe. Crying, laughing, breathing—she held her belly. Crouched in this too tight closet that was used to house bottles of pungent cleansers and buckets of stale water, she was getting her air back. Breathing. She saw the ringing trees and the sun breaking through above. The Clearing. It replaced the cleansers and mops as she gazed around Miss Mary's space. Breathing. Breathing. Breathing.

For Auntie

Kisaye Natsuki

I never called you Mother, but mother you
were
to
me
especially, lost from the
arms and womb, of the
body that ushered me in to
the world, you
were there
lost too.
I
never called you mother, mama,
auntie, you were,
and yes, you were
my
Auntie, Everyone
knew me as
your
child
but ...
you.
The unnamed threat between us
sang a hymn no one could hear
but
feel
undercurrent to our every
day
we felt it, in the waves at night, the crashing darkness that masks
dusks' travel to dawn
Wide, as the
ocean
that we paid homage to on as many
Saturdays as we could Skipping
over waves, that graced us too,
as
tumultuous blankets beneath our bronzed bodies like bound bamboo
our bellies flat while arms played sail,
navigating
balance The cousins,

running up and down the
stretches of
shore
line framed with black
rocks like small mountains
echoing the big mountain
road we drove up on as
wide as this
it
was, the threat
that, you would
lose me.
my
color, a reminder in this sea
of shades categorized by
value that bore us all to
ask
who we
were to
each
other
Master of our bond.
I
try to revive, a memory, older
than this in my desire, for
you. But the sea, is too wide
the threat, too big
filled with your own longings, long abandoned like
the old house we lived in before, the one closer to
the sea. Its discarded boards on shore. Long before,
me.
Now, only the faded indigo
collapsing sky above the night
waves' crashing in hymn holds us
close
as, you
struggle to love me,
This child, placed in your arms,
mother
lost at sea,
Bosom absent,
Mother
of mine.

Supernova

Victoria Moten

I lost my mom last April and bought a telescope to try to find her. When I was little I believed stars were affixed to the sky. Like water droplets on the window after a good rain, just there adding texture to the view. My mom believed in heaven, freedom, peace. What could be more peaceful then the silence of space? More free than the boundlessness of the universe? Was this not heaven to a terrestrial being like me?

My sister claims to be haunted by her. That her ghostly figure lingers in the rooms of our childhood home. I guess I hope that she finally broke free of this world and ran as fast as she could away from it. But then again, I guess I'm also jealous. How come she hasn't visited me? How come I have to go searching? Is it because I wasn't a good daughter? How I long to hear the voice that was silenced by a stroke a month before her departure. My last words to her, "I can't hear you, can you just text me?"

Dad made a shrine around her ashes. He brings her flowers every Friday and talks to her as if she never left. My mom used to tell us to give people their flowers while they're here to appreciate them. I think my father's ritual is to atone for not heeding that advice. He keeps her plants watered and took the flowers that people bring to your house when they don't know what to say to the widow and built an indoor garden filling the spaces where my mother once walked.

I cried for a week after my fiddle leaf died. Tried everything to keep it alive, but it was too late. Something about seeing it slowly gray, as its veins stuck out giving its last few pulses until it finally wilted triggered the memory of watching my mom as she took her last breath in her hospital bed.

She was tired. Sick and tired. As most of us are. Tired of the world beating us down. Tired of smiling through the burdens of fear, stress, pain, and shame. On my last visits with her I massaged her feet because she was in so much pain. I remember begging the nurses to bring the pain relievers but they shuffled their feet and took hours to finally get to her. As if she didn't matter. But she mattered to us. She didn't go a day without a visitor, but no one else seemed to care. She was tired. Sick and tired and lived in the juxtaposition most of us do–of wanting to be both carried for a little while and stand on our own two feet. For a long while I was angry but I didn't know who to direct the anger to. Her late stage Cancer diagnosis was a surprise to us, but I wondered if pride kept her from telling us or if the doctors never got around to telling her. When she took her last breath, did she leave us or did they let her go? I will never know.

But what I do know as I peer through the mirrors looking deep into the abyss, is that like a supernova, her departure tore the fabric of my universe. But now I have my own little moon orbiting my world. How will I ever explain to him that a star that no longer dots the sky, dictates the tilt of my axis? That every time I cornrow his hair or kiss him goodnight or sing to him that those small acts are the remnants of the stardust his grandmother left behind? That she was my sun—radiant and giving all of her light to her daughters? I ask these questions in the mirror, studying her face, light years away.

When Someone You Know Dies by Suicide Again

Maya Williams (after Camonghne Felix)

You recognize how it hurts to admit how often
Suicide has a point. If Suicide is a solution
to a temporary problem, why must the problem become permanent as
punishment to continue to live? A youth attempts to sign Suicide's offer with a
bedsheet the paper and the gasps from his windpipe the ink, a C.O. coos, Do
it. A trans woman drives home from a peer support group, exhaling exhaustive
signatures, you will never know the full complexity of the forces that convince
her, Do it. The same week an adult chooses to stay tearing his contract to
shreds, a different adult chooses to leave. What made one Do it stronger than
the other?

Survivor's Guilt is a stone
thrown to your sternum each time you live
longer than your loved ones. You wish the stone would hurt you enough to
want to join your loved ones, and you feel even worse than all the stones can
do is hurt. You aren't in the same headspace as your loved ones were right
now. Yes, that is a good thing; and it isn't enough to numb the bruises or the
breaking of your bones. No, this does not discount the loved ones who still
choose to live alongside you. You swear you are grateful for their bandages.

You remind yourself that there are more people
alive now
then anyone in the past who has died.

You remind yourself of how there are humans
doing better
at convincing you and more to stick around.

Day 3

Felicia Johnson

On the downward spiral
of my dark moon cycle
purple dreams
twist and turn
in the lit up night
my stomach churns
on bittersweet prayers
apple turnover nightmares
and too much rum...
redeeming myself at face value
i underbid on this lovely
reflection
ran a boston and almost
lost the game
with my always-winning hand.
i didn't count my dubplates
while the children set the turntables
so now i'm two plates short
hungry
tired
making forward motion
on a backwards promise
believing in the fool's dream
that pyrite backs up these dollars
that eggs cure loneliness
that He brought me this far
to drop me
into this land of

dusty cornrows and belligerent housewives.
zombies in the daytime.
music playing in my head all the time.
You Can't Stop Thiiiissss
downward spiral of my dark moon cycle
i slip and slide
in the primordial waterpark
of loooove
infinite
precious and delicate
i land on the not-too-nice side of the ocean
heart throbbing
oozing and cut
by the jagged edges of Egun's dream...

Why We Nod at Each Other (A folktale)

Meilan Carter-Gilkey

Three rivers, well two rivers and one stream, braided together, slowly and then rushing, with a current bouncing along the banks, that fell over the edge into a pool, that spilled and fanned like hair spread out on a fresh pillow. It was in this pool, where the waters were dark and thick, that the people lost their reflections. The reflection of the sunlight against their skin was almost blinding with shades of coppery brown, golden sand, red clay and rich sable. It was difficult to stare deeply into the shimmering light so they nodded at each other in recognition. Long necks held baskets and clay vessels without a quiver, tools in strong grips, gourds and roots carried for trade and babies straddled to ample hips or tied to backs, covered in the song of their ancestors, they spoke with their eyes and moved as one.

No one could recall when the humming began, because it felt like it had always been there. Causing ripples in the pool, the melody grew loud enough that the people across the water stopped singing. They cocked their heads to listen, to find the source. The people followed the sound, growing louder in the center of the water. Their steps into the water were steady, almost in time with the music. Gliding as if hypnotized, they began humming, not feeling the water rising up their thighs. Suddenly the drums began, or maybe they had always been there? The steady beat clashed with the new song on their tongues; the rhythmic vibrating pulsing like a warning cry, but it was too faint for them to be certain. So distracted overwhelmed they were that they could not hear clearly the cries or the drummers' message to retreat, tapped out on goat skin heads, ri-tat-tat, ri-tat-tat-tat, ri-tat-tat, ri-tat-tat-tat, it was too late to turn around. They were standing with water lapping against their navels, against stretch marks that spooled out life stories, before seeing their reflections swallowed into the water like a whirlpool of melted colors. They were muted, unable to call to each other with mouths or their eyes. As they sank into the murky water, sludge covered their shine, and camouflaged their skin. An arm, a leg or a foot disfigured or missing when they returned to the surface.

First they gasped for air and then they gasped for the horror of their new silhouettes; humped backs, mutated fingers, white glowing eyes and every heart hidden behind an empty chamber, their heartbeats now inaudible, but they heard the ri-tat-tat-tat, ri-tat-tat, ri-tat-tat. As the beats shook the mud floor, they understood. They listened to the drums' language, replaced it with their missing heartbeats: ri-tat-tat-tat, ri-tat-tat, ri-tat-tat. It called them, drowning out the hum, ri-tat-tat-tat, ri-tat-tat, ri-tat-tat, from that space beneath the waterfall. The elders greeted them at the fall's gates, staring at the disfigured bodies and showing the young ones their own missing pieces. They beckoned them to follow as the elders stepped under the sheet of the waterfall. The rhythm of the drums changed, it slowed as the young ones, mute, broken, and bent, parted the curtain of water. As soon as the water streamed over their bodies, glints of copper, sable, red clay and sand sparkled under the mud.

The deeper the people moved into the cave, the faster the sludge melted away and their skin shined in its natural hues along their fully shaped bodies. Then the elders smiled quietly as the young ones rejoiced at their original reflections and a few noticed the elders no longer looked twisted and covered with scars. The people bowed their thanks to the drummers and the musicians nodded in return. From the darkest part of the cave came a voice, with a power too strong for the aging frail shell of the singer. The mournful melody captured every feeling in the eyes of the people. Every person present nodded to the song, some cried and all mourned and understood that this was now their only sacred space. One young child stood on the edge outside of the group and she scanned the faces, still in awe. She turned back, to stick her palm through the cascading water foaming around her feet, and her palm grew cold, her fingers unrolled into a shadow imitating hooked claws with a missing thumb. The girl lost her breath as she yanked her hand back and watched her flesh and thumb reappear. As she turned from the falls, she saw the people gather closer as she walked towards them. They embraced her with open faces and each pair of eyes met hers, while the elder sang on. Because under the falls could they clearly see her.

From that day that on, our people wore the skins of fear above the surface. Those above the water only saw the distortion, under the water, they shined brightly and the others who saw them had to stay submerged and hold their breath. You see our true reflections can only be seen under waterfalls and in the eyes of each other. And this, dear ones, is why we nod and greet one another.

Emotional Junkfood

Rowana Abbensetts-Dobson

You are my favorite emotional junk food,
My fingers are sticky with your voice,
You cling to my teeth like sweet toffee.
Leave salt on my lips like powder dusted chips,
You give me temporary delirium,
shiny packaging, artificial flavors
You're so bad, it's good.
Handful after handful, I cannot stop.
Although I know I should go,
Your flowers are so deceptive,
I don't feel my teeth rot,
I don't feel my stomach churn,
Or my blood pressure rise,
I don't notice the extra inch on each thigh,
My mind in a stupor, I surrender to malaise.
And dream of you, a slow lick ice cream cone
On a sweaty summer day.
The doctor says you'll be the death of me,
But how can poison give such unbridled glee?
You are my favorite emotional junk food,
Hidden in cupboards for emergencies and safe keeping.
You are love that feels like pain,
that looks like a Black girl weeping.

All the Benches in Manhattan Have Ghosts in Their Wood

Chelsea Williams

All the Benches in Manhattan Have Ghosts in Their Wood
I am some kind of magnet, he says
I have a way of snake charming
boys that I meet who want to tell me
about their mothers and their last meal
the desires and deals they tuck in prayers on Sunday
I stir the incense of their emotions
we meet on the cross roads of a map
going in separate directions atop a gallery of glass boxes
he looks like a Tupac mixture
spiral lashes thick brows a flower pierced
through his nose, a reptile hanging from his ear
he holds the door open for strangers
bows to women we meet
I am not sure if this is just to impress me but
here I am reminded that I can be (desired) (fooled)
here I am swept in the Thursday afternoon air
held on an arm through the park, he says
I look like a girl that reads, I look like
a chlorophyll rose, I look like
a girl you lose in a crowd
he asks when will we meet again?
I know something he doesn't -
I am a page sewn between chapters,
dust catching him under the nose
content with disappearing
I lean into strange boys
trying to cast enchantments on me
I am not long for any of their worlds
I am good at loving in transit,
I lean into their shoulders
then fade into mist shadows

You

Whylde Chylde

What is it with you?
And the way you cross my mind.
It starts as feeling;
Tightness in my chest,
To match the tightness between my thighs
Heart pumping and the pressure building

Aware of the blood
Flowing through my veins
To the warmth that is me.
Just ready,
With the images of you.
And feelings of you give me.

Fighting the urge
To give in
Straight into you.
Always knowing the feeling that comes after,
What I have lost,
And whatever else that follows.

Gushing
With pure energy
Rawness
And passion.
The natural ebb and flow
It's the ride to our climax

The product
Of your pleasure
Littered through my brain
A mind field
Of my nerve receptors
Triggered by the thoughts of you.

Janet Jackson Wants to Dance with Me

Suzi Q. Smith

today
I want to dance with you
because

yesterday
I saw some footage
from the traffic camera
of you

offering the afternoon rush hour
the strongest seat-belted choreography
ever performed

while you sang the words
   when I was seventeen
   I did what people told me
and the shoulder leans
and the shimmy into the steering wheel
and back again

I could see
your second-grade self
finally got what she wanted
   Got my own mind
   I want to make my own decisions
   When it has to do with my life, my life
   I wanna be the one in control

and once
I watched you perform your version of
That's the Way Love Goes
to a full house
at the Walnut Room
in a vest
and a beaded necklace
and at least three men
wanted to propose
and I love
that dedication

and on New Year's Eve in 2017
you and your homegirls
stared into the small screen
on your iPhone because
you wanted to study
the perfection of movement
in Rhythm Nation
and for a moment
the people of the world did unite
and you were
that night
for sure
a part
of the Rhythm Nation

and when the break on If drops
you dance with a furious precision
elbows sharp and hips dropped
while you imagine all the loves who lost you
and the time last week
when the DJ cut the track
before the break
you almost cussed him out

and mostly
I want to dance with you
because you've been offering me
your precious sweat
since 1980 something
and still do the snake
when you hear
What Have You Done for Me Lately

because
like me
you dance a little
every day
just to remember
you can move
and be moved
and is that not
why we
are here?

The Floral Pedestal

Shamoiya Washington

Adults need their hand held too when they cross the street
Protect them,
watch over them,
look out for any danger that may come their way.

Shower them with love, kisses, hugs – the endless affection that they
once knew
Turn them into mush
Make them feel silly inside with your ridiculous expressions and gestures
Allow them to get excited, to share their new muses with you.

Let them experience your tenderness,
rock them ever so gently,
and graze your thumb against the bottom of their wet cheek
Inspire them to believe again
Nurture what you want to see in them

Some Old Havoc

Ciera Javae

A Golden Shovel After Eve L. Ewing

I'm a resurrected dialect/ a mosaic tongue	i
Was found overboard sleeping on an ocean floor by which I	mean
I'm deadly/ biblical locust/ hungry for your firstborn sons	you
Have no words for this kind of reckoning & I	can't
Dumb it down for you/ by which I mean my name is a	spell
To conjure the clicks & cadence of tribes once subsided cause see	anything
Is a Mississippi March waiting to happen again and again and	I
Am honest by which I mean I will wreak havoc on forefathers & fickle men/	talk
About the lives I've lived in this body/	about
Stono, Nat, Toussaint, Herbert, Gabriel and Cudjo	with
Weapons, words, waters too little to drown our griots	that
Is what is forgotten/ that the griot lives/ ascends into a new tongue never	sorry
For existing in a world unrecognizable by your	alphabet
Too rudimentary for the likes of me, mammy, jezebel, sapphire, and	you
Forget I'm a gladiolus, by which I mean I grow long and wide in dirt and still	have
The audacity to glisten like there is nothing	left
But a mutiny at my thighs begging for it to be	over
By which I mean the flag free of blood but Black	from
The cliché of berries/ a grandma's gospel and the ascension of the last slave ship on	yesterday

PART III:
REST INTIMACY GRIEF

In Memoriam: Rev. Martin Luther King, Jr. (Part I)

June Jordan, Soulscript

honey people murder mercy U.S.A
The milklad turn to monsters teach
To kill to violate pull down destroy
The weakly freedom growing fruit
From being born

America

tomorrow yesterday rip rape
exacerbate despoil disfigure
crazy running threat the
deadly thrall
appall belief dispel
the wildfire burn the breast
the onward tongue
the outward hand
deform the normal
rainy riot sunshine
shelter wreck of darkness
derogate delimit blank
explode deprive
assassinate and batten up
like bullets fatten up
the raving greed
reactive a springtime
terrorizing
duplication death
by death by men by more
than you or I can
STOP

I am

Ariel Ward

may child
born
elusive
like dreams
at dawn
i am

protected
a stare
you cannot break
a moving spirit
i am

spring mornings
silky soft like sunrise dew
a petite flower
at half bloom
i am

a dance
feet that sway
to scattered melodies
a tender waltz
i am

everything
i thought i knew
the best things
my best thing
i am

the breath of air
that escaped deaths gasp

black magic
black woman
i am

an answer
a soundful prayer
humming gently
the hymns of my
grandmother
i am

an ancestral conjure
delicate and defiant

nothing less
than a wonder

i am

"If I didn't define myself for myself, I would be crunched
into other people's fantasies for me and eaten alive."
— Audre Lorde

A Recipe for Exhale C.A.K.E.[1]

dr. adrienne danyelle oliver

I. *Ingredients*

1 part acceptance that you are like mamma
       wrapped up in deathless regenerative flesh
1 tsp becoming balm to the throughline
       of mammas from whence you came
2 parts letting go of the throughline
       of mammas from whence you came
3 parts stepping into
       your own power
2 dashes of as it was and so it shall be
1 cup of prayer
3 scoops of ashe
a pinch of namaste
1 dollop of amen
      ~*selah* to taste

II. Instructions

Gather three beautiful mixing bowls made of heart-whole
Preheat belly to forgiveness degrees oversoul
     in first bowl
         mix 1 part acceptance + becoming balm
            let stand until the mixed-upness gels into calm
      in a second bowl
         mix   letting go + ashe
              namaste + ashe
      and knowing it will be okay
                 and
      seeing into the future again
            let the okayness soak all the way in

in a third bowl
         combine all ingredients into the as it was and so it shall be
           blend until the mix is a smooth consistency

---

1   Conscious All-Knowing Essence

stir
pour
bake
set the alarm for cosmic hours
this will help those throughlines rise to full ancestral power

bake until you see the batter[ed] rise
like oil wells pumping in hips and
diamonds at meeting of thighs
once prayer, ashe, and namaste has into day risen
cool with a sprinkling of amen and let acceptance into the kitchen
instead of the counter for cooling, put this on the highest rack
countering ain't worth the stepping time in the beat you've risen at
garnish with baby's breath
to add wonder and   awe (~*selah*) to taste
step into your power and

                              in joy

                                    your exhale C.A.K.E.

My Exhale Releases the Pain

Sonnie Dae

There's a part of me that calls me blame
Hijacks my brain
Says: 'I'm lame'
a sad, denigrating refrain
Stresses and strains
And calls me names
Plaques me with guilt, doubt, and shame

In this moment,
I choose to remain
calm, safe, at peace, and sane—
steadying this rocky terrain

Through my exhale, I release the pain
Knowing 'This too shall pass'

Little Sorrow

Danielle Shaleece

They say nine blackbirds got they wings clipped last night
that them blackbirds was trying to reach heaven with they prayers
that some white man gunned them down
I say them blackbirds never had wings in the first place
that even though Kendrick say blackbird

fly

them blackbirds wings stay trampled on and
held down them ain't really wings anyway
blackbirds ain't got no wings
ain't got no fly
when white boys can kill them
and stay alive.
Evermore by

Evermore

Alie Jones

after Sonia Sanchez

This is not a small voice
You hear
This is a resounding symbol
Bombas and maracas
This is the song of those who
Chose the sea
Those who wanted better for
You and
Me
This is not a small voice
You hear
This a familiar hum
Your great
Great grandmothers drum
Sending shivers
up your vertebrae
And down
Your meridian
This is not a small heart
You see
This a big heart
Swelling with love
Buoyant as the sea
Demanding transformation
Calling in healing and restoration
Together

Carolina Gold Mississippi Blue (3)

Constance Collier-Mercado

—after Vievee Francis

There are voices in my head that won't let
me claim my people. Guilt seeds the

idea they're not mine to hold. There's a river
cross my tongue ripe with colors I carry

to paint myself whole. Blue gold shades me
one-third praise hymn two-thirds contradiction. Like:

Plantation named for the place he stole us from - a
misnomer. Like: Me saying us when one is but a shell

of the other - or so the voices steady scold. How to
halt such Great River Road division. Unknown.

What happens to a people after flood waters
subside. Divide. I was born in Illinois, let

the records tell it. Came alive the day they told me
about 1927. Reminded of 37-73-93-2011. Could be

I am of this blood if not from this land. Filled
to bursting, each vein a levee filled to bursting, with

salt and swamp and stubborn grit to survive another
day. Could be I'll play those numbers anyway. Spirit

shifts from guilt to saving grace. I have earned this
Black like the conjure before me. When it is time

to teach take my winnings and buy back each one.
Memory sheds its raw husk. Not so strange as that

chorus of beavers and geese on display but a will,
wild as the wreckage of Floyd and Florence, to see

such scatter of noble pasts give voice to an ending and
bound line of beginnings which only Dahomey could abide.

When I Stopped Running From My Mother I Exhaled

Jeanine DeHoney

When I was a child, I used to run away from my mother. I thought it was a game at first, watching her chase behind me until she became exasperated, breathless, as she called my name, "Jeanine, come back here." I was oblivious to how that stopped her very breath, and she only exhaled when she wrapped me in her arms.

I was around age six or seven years old. One time I remember I had a painful earache. My mother rushed me to the hospital emergency room. After we sat in the crowded waiting room for a long time after getting checked in, my pain lessened. Bored, I ventured off before my mother could stop me, running down the long sterile white corridors of the hospital.

Within seconds although it felt much longer, this Black warrior woman, holding the black leather purse she carried like an appendage of her body everywhere because it held her important documents, swooped me up to her bosom with her other hand, her own eyes misty, making me promise to never run away from her again.

Nonetheless like an insolent child I didn't listen, not knowing the fear that rose in her spirit every time I ran from her. I kept running thinking it was a game. I unloosed her hand from mine and darted across the street as cars came to a screeching halt. Or I wandered away from her when we were at the supermarket or shopping for clothes.

Thankfully I grew out of running away from my mother physically as I got older. But during my awkward tween and teenage years, my running away transformed into silent treatments and closed doors towards her, and it continued even when that stage passed, and I became an adult, and later a wife and mother.

I shut my voice down to the woman who loved me intensely and unconditionally and whom I should have taken cliff notes from to chart my way through each stage of womanhood and motherhood. Somehow, I couldn't let go of my impulse to take flight.

I think back to those times and wish I could take them all back. How I chose my closed bedroom instead of making room for her, this beautiful black woman who gave me life? How could I grow mute with the woman who gave me my voice…who taught me my first words? How could I not give her the greatest gift, so simple and free of cost, that she wanted, to have a close mother/daughter/and later grown black woman relationship now that I was in that season of my life.

I think back to those times and wish I hadn't hung something over her head for so long, something I didn't talk with her about until years later. If I had, I know that breathless feeling my mother carried, from chasing after a daughter that ran from her, would have ceased and she would have had the sweet release of an exhalation. We both would have much sooner.

Although it was nothing traumatizing that I held against my mother. It still pulled at the tightly woven threads of our relationship as I got older. I was disheartened that my mother never went after her dreams.

My mother was a stay-at-home mother but from the time I was a child I heard stories from my grandmother and aunts, and even herself, about how she wanted to be both a singer and a psychiatrist. As a child and as a teenager she sang on a local radio station. My grandmother who loved spirituals used to say she had a songbird's voice. And because she loved helping people and giving advice, my mother wanted to be a psychologist and had even gone to college for a few semesters to pursue it, but stopped once she got married to my father, who was an aspiring jazz musician.

She believed in my father's dreams I think more than her own, and would often accompany him to Harlem jazz clubs and house parties to watch him play until she became pregnant with my older sister. But my father's own wounds from the past, and later health problems caused him to stop playing. He pawned his golden saxophone, to pay some mounting bills, and got a civil service job while my mother raised my sister and I fulltime and took care of my grandmother.

Although there were innumerable pluses for my sister and I that came with her being a stay-at-home mother, the truth is I wished she had pursued her dreams, even one of them. It troubled me that in the same breath of calling my mother's name that I couldn't jokingly but proudly add doctor to it or I couldn't get to see her perform some soul stirring song on stage.

My mother's singing would have stirred up someone's heart and she would have been an awesome psychologist. For the latter she held all the traits for being one; empathy, and wisdom I like to say from our ancestors. She had been here before soul.

My mother was likewise a dreamcatcher for my sister and I. She reminded us we could be anything in the world, and to never let anyone tell us differently because of our skin-color. But she hadn't laid the blueprint out for us on how to do that. Even though others did like my aunt and other female kin, (one opening a storefront real estate agency, and another selling Avon and Mary Kay while working a fulltime job as a single mother) I still longed to witness it…inhale it like a "how to" fragrance from my own mother so I would have known the ebbs and flows of my own dream journey, the good and the bad, once I went after it.

Sometimes when I caught her in quiet moments of introspection, I wondered what was it that stopped her from going back to realize her dreams even when we were school age? Had her dreams been so far pushed into the alcoves they no longer seemed feasible to her or did she just sacrifice them so that she could make sure my sister and I attained ours? And although I'll be forever indebted to her for her sacrifices, it dings at my heart because as a writer I can't imagine not ever writing. If I stopped, I'd be submerged in a sadness that rose from my gut and cut off my air supply until I picked up my pen again.

It wasn't until my thirties that I decided to talk about my feelings with my mother so I could stop running away emotionally from her. Although we had never stopped talking, I called her every day, I wanted to peel back the onion skin to have a deeper conversation. I knew I loved her from a tighter "heart place" than she deserved. And I knew it was time to oil the squeaks in our relationship.

It was in the quietness of my mother's kitchen, my childhood home, as we drank cups of tea, hers always with a splash of canned milk and two sugar substitutes to my honey and lemon in mine, that we talked on a profounder level. We talked not just as a mother and daughter but as two grown women about life, love and black womanhood, our fears, our hopes and our dreams. And when asked why she didn't follow hers, she said that dreams change and she wouldn't have traded being there for me and my sister for anything.

I had to accept that. That my mother's choice was her own and she stood ten toes down with it. Learning to accept that helped me to become unbound from my false narrative of her and why she gave them up. It helped me finally exhale so my breath could become sacrosanct with hers, finally.

When I look at old photographs of my mother, I can tell she was happy. She was happy encouraging, and inspiring others and happy making her black daughters feel invincible in a world they would have to have the strength of an oak tree to maneuver in.

My voice is her voice, tinged with empathy for others. My writing is because of her, and me sitting at her knee as a child, watching her write in notebooks that I mirrored. My activism is because of her because I remember those times, she sat in front of our apartment building with other women tenants registering others to vote, or getting them to sign petitions for better community services, or how she took my sister, best friend, and I to see Mama Africa, the late South African singer, songwriter, civil-rights activist and apartheid advocate, Miriam Makeba, when I was around eleven or twelve years old.

My empathy towards others, sometimes to a default, is all her. My words and gestures are lined up with her words, especially her favorite ones like…" This too shall pass." "Or trust your gut," "Don't be no one's fool," "A watched pot never boils," or just a reassuring "You got this."

How many times have I passed those same black Mama sayings on to my children, my kin, my sister friends? And with the same gesticulations as her…hands moving, head cocked to the side, or hands gently stroking the hand of the recipient of her words.

My mother is no longer alive to run towards to so she can wrap her arms around me as warmly as a patchwork quilt. But I am so at peace that she knew years before her earthly body left this earth that I loved her fervently, that I was proud of her, and that I would never want her to change who she was because who she was, was the best part of her and now me.

It is because of her that I can walk through any darkness, any fire, any storm unnerved, holding on to my crown, and exhale, breathe in and breathe out I take to center myself… knowing as my mother would say, "This too shall pass," and "You got this."

Jan 24

Karla Brundage

Crying spontaneously in random places
My heart leaps when memory, my mind corners
Under a swing we are falling in love
The look in your eyes when you, my toes touch
A scent of strawberries and coke remains
Down my soft coat darkness now tumbles
Facing the ocean -where suddenly tumbles,
An aching memory of special places
Where once we stood and loved -remains
Photos of that day now stacked in corners
My face close to yours I long to touch
Razor stubble and call you, my love
Suddenly you had stopped your love
Like a glass that from a shelf tumbles
What happened in that last finger touch
When you knew my secret places
I let you enter, all those corners
And now only your shadow remains
Red sled I bought for your son remains
Lodged in my memory of our lost love
I find pieces of you in many corners
And in those moments tears they tumble
Fear grips me passing those places
Where your warmth I used to touch
When did I lose my touch
The one that could convince you to remain
I seek you in so many places
Wondering where I lost my love
My mind circles, I cannot turn that corner
When will my memories of you tumble?
Corners of our love are what remains
Touching me when I try new love
Tumbles me in to terrifying places

My Marrow

Asantewaa Boykin

My marrow
Remembers
Mississippi
New Orleans
Benin
Project jungle gyms
Nooses
Violated peace treaties
That put cousins
On slave ships
Songs
Sung
At crossroads
Riverbanks
Oceans
Prisons gates
It's funny
But
Not

Me and
Granny
I mean
"Grandma"
Are still bargaining
For new backs

Both choosing motherhood
Believing we should
But perhaps
Should have chosen - the globe
France in spring
White men
Abstract paintings
And black magic
But as time would have it
We both choose
Not to chose

WE MOVE TO MILITANT LOVE, DON'T WE?

Daad Sharfi

after Gordon Parks' Untitled photograph taken in Watts, California, 1967

They don't want us smiling

flashing all of our teeth into a brand-new weapon

don't want our mouths stretched wide *Oh!*pen

brown hands prying apart the sky

by the spine--disk by desk, we uncolumn

its nerves & state our names

into the next day's darkening.

Every day, we fashion a portal through which we fly

& our mistakes don't follow.

Chins up & compass-like, pointing in the direction

of the Heavens or

our people's People--whichever comes first.

If they don't want us smiling,

imagine how they feel about

our singing,

& our carrying on--

how we tend to broken skin with salves

sent from somewhere holy

If they don't want us smiling,

imagine how they feel

about our asking one another:

Did you get free today?

I am the river

Raychelle Heath

I am the river   I am the riverbed   I am the longing that left here
I am the curve in the mountain's side   I am the smoothed stone   I am the exhale that
released the pebble in your throat
I am the after of the drowning I am a moment between teeth
you cannot hold me I am not possible this way
I am the final tear that remembers you that held your breath so gently in the palm of a
cloud that rained you into the riverbed
I am reborn
I am lush green reaching for drink I am an amalgam I am clay I am muddy waters–
the bottom of a steel cup deep dregs still fragrant with caramel and mountains
the mountain's curve dances on my surface I hold it in my reflection trees close in
rain breaks the surfaces where are the tadpoles the moving moments that
remember me the time weathered in a porch swing the song of the chain
I remember the way you dissolved into a small soft thing like so much spun sugar in a
storm
the colors run I can't hold you you are not possible that way
how do human hands reconstruct a cloud to be more than a clumsy replica of a piece of
heaven
I have no mind for that only the duty of this body to push push push through the work
that
flows and flows and flows
be present stay with the current or you will drown exhaust yourself into the riverbed
the riverbed knows you but won't tell

untitled futures

shah noor hussein

black queer sudan is
wandering the street sans *hijab*
is me locks out
piercings visible
tattoos on display

black queer sudan is
is wearing pants to the wedding
and lipstick too
is saying yes or no to *henna*
and deciding for yourself
which side of the *salah* to sit in
and going back and forth between both

black queer sudan is
is going back and forth between both

black queer sudan is
sneaking cigarettes and booze
on my grandmother's rooftop
trying to explain to my male cousin that i'm gay
by talking about Black feminism
and my lack of interest in marriage
and all the qualities that put me in opposition
to compulsory heteronormativity

"i don't cook good"
"i won't clean up after him"
"i will want to wander alone"
"i will want to wander"
"i will want alone"
"i will want—"

black queer sudan is
sneaking a out of my aunties with my cousin
both of us in a mission to talk to our boos
and knowing mine was a woman
and knowing mine was a queer
and knowing mine was—

black queer sudan is
my uncle crossing his legs defiantly
when asked about marriage
proclaiming –
"it sounds like unwanted labor to me"

black queer sudan
is my *khaltu* rejecting men's proposals
while waiting for that "one"
who could either not offer what she wanted,
or didn't want it as deeply, in the same way

black queer sudan is
me at the *skeihs* house
and trying not to squirm
unsure of what was happening around me
and craving to tap in

black queer sudan is
salwa's smirk
at the center of my frame
consuming my role / roll
is the way i wonder
about that smile even now
and how i took everyone's picture
just to get hers

duality

Kimani Rose

peaches
mangos

fried catfish
menudo

I have maiden names in Martinez and Honor
in Hamilton and Samuels

I knew how to roll my r's
I knew how to eat a tamale without getting the rib sauce on it
collard greens separate from los plátanos fritos y empanadas de calabazas

we are the fruit of our mothers
peaches and mangos hanging from sweet healthy trees
we are homelands on boats

peaches because the there's no records before chains touched sand
mangos because somewhere
la abuela de mis antepasados puts her hands in warm soil and plants us
in homes away from homes
places i will never go

and maybe Mother Earth is an angry Black woman, too

Mallessa James

And maybe Mother Earth is
an angry Black woman,
too.
Maybe she's tired of her historical role
playing mammy to those who would oppress her,
who act like they own her –
Objectifying her for their own convenience,
fighting over her for their own power,
stealing from her for their own gain,
selling her labors for their own profits,
abusing her body for for their own pleasure,
destroying her family for their own entertainment –
Who feel justified treating her
like she's a piece of property.
Maybe she just can't take it anymore.
So when it gets to be too much,
she lets go of everything she's been holding back –
Glaring with a scorching heat or
whispering with a bitter cold,
exploding into a fiery rage or
unleashing a torrent of tears,
cursing up tornadoes of pain or
screaming out hurricanes of grief –
Because she is more than ready
to teach these fools a lesson.
Maybe she is thinking
about how she brought humanity into this world,
and how she can take us out of it,
too.
And maybe she knows –
One way or another,
with or without us,
today or a thousand years from now –
She has the power within her to
transform all the scars,
transmute all the poisons,
transcend all the traumas,
and start her life over
again.

In Memoriam

Maya Williams

after Jenny Boully

Not a casket, but an urn
Not an urn, but an ornament Not
an ornament, but a memory Not a
memory, but a door Not a door,
but a window Not a window, but
a breeze Not a breeze, but a sigh
Not a sigh, but a sunray
Not a sunray, but a rain cloud
Not a rain cloud, but a bed Not
a bed, but a wound
Not a wound, but a sore
Not a sore, but a hug
Not a hug, but a gaze
Not a gaze, but a breath
Not a breath, but an ending Not
an ending, but a beginning

Processing Grief: A Meditation
RR Scott

I invite you into this sacred space. A space where you can be you. A space where you can process. This has been a time of collective grief and individual grief. I invite you to be vulnerable at this pace.

Breathe in

Breathe out

(Speak these words aloud or silently)

It is hard to unlearn the lessons that were passed down from great great grandmother to great grandmother to grandmother to mother to you. For protection, they taught us to suppress. To suppress joy and pain. Especially pain to keep one safe. It is hard to lean into feeling the full joy. The full love. The full anger. Grief is heavy. And they knew that.

Inhale.

Exhale.

You live in this world where it is safe to long in silence. Where it is not quite safe to love loudly. To get angry fully. To let the tears fall uninhabited.

Inhale.

Exhale.

And sometimes you still have to move with caution to fit into a space that will not let you be as you are. And this makes you feel angry. Sad. Frustrated. Incredulous.

The repressed joy.

The unrequited love.

And when you feel, you feel a tug deep in your soul but not a fullness. So you still struggle with feeling like you deserve to experience full happiness. Even in times of great passion, you're muted. In times of great anger, you instead let it simmer. In times of sorrow, you hold steady. To be the backbone. Grief is heavy.

Inhale.

Exhale.

Are you safe right now? In your own space.

Can you carve out a small space to be? To grieve?

Sit there. Stand there. Lie there. Be there in that safe space.

Inhale.

Exhale.

Be still.

Invoice

Joyce Lee

To:	The World
From:	A Black Womyn
Business:	The way I want, I deserve on bended knee, praising apologies since the day before I created myself a secret swimming from my daddy's pleasure.
Name:	My granny already prayed the world's entire debt. Blessed me to be the one to bring the world the bill.
Service:	I have rested a bit on the cotton picked, enjoyed the tobacco, whiskey until after drunk, fat & busting. Numerous nights I learned patience in pig fat salving bloodied white meat, vertebrae thrashed, gaping with the sick pleasures of others: The hot piss of the church, the tar & feather of this regime, men of all hues trying to shove their dicks inside of the moribund gash in my back saying my skin begged for the extra slit why else would it rip so melodically for their pre-exonerated invasions?!
Taxes:	Many miles endured a parched endurance, so long at Love's feet, in hopes to prove I too am most worthy at Love's side! I deserve to bathe in sensual tears too! Be Loved without being conquered. To be held while strong bended knees until bloodied if need be! Heart ripped from one's own ribcage in hand, whole vascular in full *signum crucis* before kissed & raised & someone bowing & willing to die in allegiance to me!
Minimum:	**I deserve sacrifice!!!**

That Time I Felt the Sun

Janae Newsom

I was walking and all the lights went out
I think I started sinking into midnight
And there were no stars
Somehow I stayed above the surface
Just enough to take
little sips of air
And then real far off in the distance
I saw something that looked like a star
And it shined and shined
Until it got so big that it became the sun
And there were no clouds
I felt adrift
Floating
Free
And it was terrifying
I knew the darkness
I knew what it felt like
I remember it's sound
I remember the way it showed no love
I remember being just above it
Enough to taste the wind
Thrashing around
Just incase it tried to sink me
But this felt like the opposite of that
And yet i was afraid because I did not want
To
Sink
Through the darkness I couldn't hear what I sounded like
Even when I screamed
And in the light I was being asked to remember
I was being asked to learn
I was being asked to grow
I was being asked to forget

Unbreakable

Kelechi Ubuzoh

I once heard,
grief is love with no place to go.
Sis, what we gonna do with this longing?

Call in your ancestors with your highest intent.
(Cuz not all ancestors are good ancestors).
Ask for guidance
ask for ease
ask for spaciousness

Request a lullaby, a fable, and a sweet memory.
Time travel through portals,
a dusty boombox will do.
Harness the power of melody.

Try the medicine of tears.
Rest.

With eyes of love,
look in the mirror.
Be seen, by you.
Speak an affirmation.
Fall in love with the miracle that is you.

Gather sadness, depression, and anger
into a room with no walls.
Ask them:
If you could release this pain, what would they dream for you? Write
down their responses,
understand their needs,
and start working on releasing.

Call a friend, a coach, a therapist, and a healer
Whoever brings you energy, sees you as whole, and knows you already have
the answers
can stay

Manifest guides not saviors.

You may feel like breaking
But you are not broken
You are not broken
You are not broken
You break open

This feeling won't last forever But
while it's here
Move through
Not around

Ask for help
And then let them help you

Tell them...'NO!'
You know who they are,
and your Black labor
Is not for sale
You are a precious being
With finite time

Rest

Create space to fall apart
Fall apart
Let yourself be held without holding Let
yourself be seen perfectly unperfect

Rest

Like a bird trapped in a building Will
find its way to sky
You will find your way to sky
There is a universe inside of your tears

Rest
Rest
Rest

You are breaking not broken
You are breaking not broken
You are not broken
You are unbreakable

In the day diamonds are in the water

Nia Pearl

After Toni Morrison

The only time the ocean cut me I bled stories.

They said
What a beautiful, yet terrifying thing it is to be free.

They said
We have traveled years to bring you our names.
*   We knew you'd forget them or worse never recognize them in the first place.*

They said
Rememory me. Unfold your tongue.
*   Gather in your hand all the cities your foremothers birthed freedom in.*
*   Scatter milkweed seeds in the wind and call Us home.*

Waterlogged and weary I bandage my wounds with diamonds
and rise from seafoam memory—homebound.

I have never been far from the page.
How else to learn what moonlight looks like through blue-eyed promises?

Oh—but to be sonia, to be toni,
to be wind in a cotton field scattering marigolds…

I wish I knew Arkansas clouds like I do the lines on a palm,
like I do the recipe for forgiveness.

Joy is memory in the refrain, magic too hopeful to stay hidden.

(The trick to befriending stories is listening after all).
Yet sometimes belonging cannot be traced by tidelines or

railroads carved out of the night sky.

But rather dogeared pages and overdue book fines. Having a library to
owe things to makes one at home, right?

So, we write, we sing, we rename our story legacy before they claim we were never here.

Find us on the page,
as She said *this* is the first battlefield we play on.

Here our words dance and so we too leap
…into blissful surrender.

And one day we will fly

and one day we will fly.

"There's a ship
The Black Freighter
With a skull on it's masthead
Will be coming in"

— Nina Simone, Pirate Jenny

Black Freighter Press publishes revolutionary books. committed to the exploration of liberation, using art to transform consciousness. A platform for Black and Brown writers to honor ancestry and propel radical imagination.